Paris by Night

PARIS BY NIGHT

David Hare

faber and faber
LONDON · BOSTON

First published in 1988
by Faber and Faber Limited
3 Queen Square London WC1N 3AU

Photoset by Wilmaset, Birkenhead, Wirral
Printed in Great Britain by
Richard Clay, Bungay, Suffolk

British Library Cataloguing in Publication Data

Hare, David
Paris by night
1. Title
822'.914   PR6058.A678
ISBN 0–571–15247–3

FOR CHARLOTTE

Introduction

Sometimes as a writer you do get a bit of luck. I had spent the greater part of 1983 struggling with the script of my first feature film. Its themes were dark and its structure was formidably complicated. So I was very much surprised to find myself back at my desk only one day after finishing it to set down a second, much simpler story which seemed to come like a free gift, an afterbirth to compensate for all the labour of *Wetherby*. It took me exactly six weeks to draft, and because it was about a Member of the European Parliament I called it *The Butter Mountain*.

For a short time *The Butter Mountain* appeared to be living a kind of charmed life, rather like the lottery ticket in René Clair's *Le Million*. I carelessly left the first script on a table in my living room, whence it was picked up, without my knowledge, by a visiting film producer. He then called me a week or two later to tell me that not only had he read it, but he had also shown it to a young man who happened at that time to be wearing the title of 'Hollywood's hottest director'. (He has since made a film, and lost it.) This young man had meanwhile showed it to Twentieth Century–Fox who were keen to do what they called 'develop' it. This would mean re-tailoring the two central roles to fit neatly into the personalities and prejudices of two fabulously well-known actors. Fox realized, of course, that such a process would necessarily be bothersome and distressing to the man who had conceived of the original idea, so they were suggesting that in return for a sum of money, paid on the nail and delivered to my bank at once, I should have nothing further to do with the project. The sum they were offering was half a million dollars.

This is, I believe, the only mephistophelean moment I have enjoyed in my writing life. All playwrights take pleasure in frightening themselves with stories of financial temptation, but in fact in England (for example, at the BBC) the sums of money involved in 'selling out' are so pitiful as to represent no very grave test of character. It was Hilaire Belloc who defined the writer's two favourite dreams as 'the return of lost loves and great sums of unexpected money'. Yet I suffered not a moment's hesitation in rejecting their offer. I might as well have been asked to sell them a child. Perhaps if I had known just how hard it would be, and how long it would take to complete the film we renamed *Paris by Night*, then perhaps I might have collected my money and fled to the hills.

I am told in Hollywood now the average period from when a film is first discussed to when the camera turns is three and a half years. *Paris by Night* took four. In peddling it round Wardour Street, I met at once with a familiar resistance. In answer to the inevitable question 'What's it based on?' I could only reply truthfully, 'Nothing. I made it up.' Films these days are so dominantly pre-digested, based on books that have been bestsellers, or little bits of newspaper that film-makers have cut out and pasted to their walls, that executives tend to come over queer when offered a script that is not based on 'facts' which they think they can hold on to. A startlingly low number of truly original screenplays now reach the screen. Once, realizing this, I bluffed a film financier by telling him that *Wetherby* was based on a story I had read in the *Yorkshire Post* about a stranger blowing his brains out in front of a schoolteacher. This blatant untruth instantly reassured him. For in the eyes of those who decide which films shall or shall not be made, there is no murkier or more unreliable place for a story to originate than inside a screenwriter's imagination.

There was a further commercial objection to *Paris by Night*, and that was of course that the leading role was written for a notably strong woman, and what's more one who was, in the cant phrase of the trade, 'unsympathetic'. Perhaps some day somebody will remember that some of the most successful films of the thirties and forties starred women doing unspeakable things, and moreover doing them with a relish to which the audience seemed ready to respond. Despairing after a year or two of seeking English finance, I went off begging in the United States, where I found an artistic orthodoxy quite as rigid as anything enforced by the commissars in Soviet Russia. On all so-called 'serious' projects (we may leave aside anything in the 'bash and slash' genre) it was an item of faith that the outcome of the story must be broadly 'optimistic' and that the leading characters must be broadly 'likeable'. It did not take me long to realize that *Paris by Night* was unlikely to be able to meet these criteria. Once, holed up in a nightmare hotel in Manhattan, I was asked by my producers to interview one of the two or three American actresses whose participation would have made the film an instant 'go'. 'I like the script,' she said, 'but I couldn't possibly play Clara Paige.' Reluctantly, I asked why not. 'Because she is so neglectful of her child.' I asked if this was something which, as an actress, she could not simulate. 'No way,' she said, showing me a lot of famous leg. 'You must understand, David, one day I'm hoping to have children myself.'

In fact it is my view that Clara Paige is not such a terrible person. Though the showbiz legislators could never admit it, she is not that different from you or me. When I went to Blackpool to see the new Tory woman, as it were, in captivity, I was struck by how much more generosity, breadth and soul I had given my principal character than was on immediate show in the simultaneously controlled and hysterical atmosphere of the annual Party Conference. Although there has been a considerable body of plays and films about the economic results of Thatcherism, there has been almost nothing of consequence about the characteristics and personalities of those who have ruled over us during these last eight years. It is one of the greatest mysteries of Thatcherism that it has generated so little fiction. In *Paradise Postponed* John Mortimer wove Leslie Titmuss into the national tapestry. But his friends and colleagues, given their eminence and power, have long seemed seriously under-represented. And no one yet seems to have written stories in which we are invited to work out just what it is these strange people want.

Somewhere in the third year of searching, the film acquired a producer, Patrick Cassavetti, who had a formidable reputation for realizing difficult projects with very little money, and somewhere in the fourth it attracted the attention of Charlotte

Rampling. I met her across a wide culture gap, made wider by a mutual ignorance of each other's work. Over lunch she praised *Wetherby* extravagantly. It was some months before I discovered she had never seen it. I was just as fulsome about *The Night Porter*, a film of which I have absolutely no memory. I also spoke well of *The Damned*, another film that I have somehow missed. After the meal, Patrick asked nervously whether we ought not perhaps to look at some of Charlotte's work before offering her the part. At the best of times reviewing an actor's earlier performances seems to me a highly doubtful and dangerous activity. If you don't know what it is that you, uniquely, want from an actor, then you should not be casting them. In Charlotte's case, a review seemed particularly pointless. She was being asked to contemplate returning to England after ten years' exile, to work with a writer and director of whom she knew very little, on a script that would show a side of herself that had scarcely been tapped in her previous career. For my part, I was guessing that under the stereotypes of mad and bad that she was usually asked to play lay a far more various and formidable actress. It was, in theory, a most spectacular gamble. And yet on a few days' acquaintance, I knew it was no gamble at all.

From the point Charlotte joined it, *Paris by Night* acquired purpose. It was no longer important it should be made. It was absolutely vital. For this reason, we went into pre-production without being properly financed, and twice faced weekends when we could not pay the wages. The first time the American producer Ed Pressman stepped in to lend us the money to carry on. The second time we ignored our problems and carried on with no money at all. Twice Patrick walked off, saying he could no longer hold the project together. I consoled him on the inevitability of his decision, but both times found him at his desk next morning. Nothing further was said. Just as the money did finally arrive, our first location was blown away in the terrible October storm. From the moment the camera turned, with the great British cinematographer Roger Pratt behind it, and a first-rate cast in front of it, I felt I was part of a team that had the power to make my writing as eloquent as possible. In the fourth week, in the Halcyon Hotel in Notting

Hill Gate, we found ourselves shooting the scene in which Clara lays out her philosophy of life to Wallace after they have made love. Clara is talking from her own experience, jumbled up with a certain amount of confused political prejudice, yet a mixture of things – the context in which she speaks, the tenderness with her lover, the play of the light, Charlotte's exquisite conviction in the role – combined to produce in those of us watching a feeling of total disorientation. We simply did not know what our response to Clara was. We were watching a woman whose head was apparently full of careless and half-thought scraps, yet in the image of her and her own self-awareness was something so moving that you could not tell if beauty was confounding truth, or if the two, as I suspect they are in life, were so mixed up that nothing could unlock them. We were all robbed of our usual reactions. This is something I have so long wanted to do as a writer that a profound and lasting contentment came upon me in that room, and it persisted through the remaining weeks of shooting. For as long as we worked, the process of art did what it has always promised: it comforted, it clarified, and set everything in order. A work and its reception are entirely different things and its making is a third. But this was one of the happiest times of my life.

DAVID HARE
March 1988

Cast and Credits

CLARA PAIGE	Charlotte Rampling
GERALD PAIGE	Michael Gambon
ADAM GILLVRAY	Robert Hardy
WALLACE SHARP	Iain Glen
PAULINE	Jane Asher
MICHAEL SWANTON	Andrew Ray
JENNY SWANTON	Niamh Cusack
SIMON	Jonathan White
JANET SWANTON	Linda Bassett
JACK SIDMOUTH	Robert Flemyng
SIR ARTHUR SANDERSON	Robert David MacDonald
LAWRENCE	Julian Firth
FOREIGN SECRETARY	Brian Cobby
YOUNG MAN	Bradley Cole
SIKH LEADER	Rashid Karapiet
SANDRA	Sandi Toksvig
DELIA	Juliet Harmer
LADY BOEING	Melissa Stribling
ENGLISH LECTURER	Peter Whitbread
FOREIGN LECTURER	Czeslaw Grocholski
SLATE-ESCOTT	Reg Gadney
MADAME ZINYAFSKI	Louba Guertchikoff
VIOLET	Tina Sportolaro
PAUL ZINYAFSKI	Alain Fromager
HECTOR ZINYAFSKI	Patrick Perez
LITTLE GIRL	Rebecca Journo
HOTEL NIGHT CLERK	Bernard Ristroph
GENDARME	Michel Motu
YOUNG HOTEL CLERK	François Greze
NURSE	Louisa Rix
GIRL AT GILLVRAY'S OFFICE	Annabel Brooks
PORTER AT CLUB	Geoffrey Wilkinson
BIRMINGHAM CHAIRMAN	Edward Clayton
BIRMINGHAM ASSISTANT	Geoffrey Larder

Director	David Hare
Producer	Patrick Cassavetti
Executive Producer	Edward R. Pressman
Film Editor	George Akers
Production Designer	Anthony Pratt
Music by	Georges Delerue
Director of Photography	Roger Pratt
Casting Director	Mary Selway
Costume Designer	Elizabeth Waller
Production Manager	Linda Bruce
Sound Recordist	Clive Winter

INT. FLAT. DAY
A close-up of a man's face lying in front of frame. He is laid out on the floor of a large mansion flat in London. He is in late middle age. His mouth is open. We take him to be dead, he is so still.

INT. HOUSE OF COMMONS: CORRIDOR. DAY
Light is thrown dramatically through Gothic windows into the dusty corridor. Sitting on a hard bench outside a private room is CLARA PAIGE. *She is in her early forties, fair-haired, businesslike, attractive. A door opens. A* YOUNG MAN *stands beside her.*
YOUNG MAN: Sir Robert will see you now. Please come in.

INT. HOUSE OF COMMONS: COMMITTEE ROOM. DAY
The FOREIGN SECRETARY *is sitting among a small group of suited men, who all face* CLARA *as she comes in. He is dark-suited, patrician. He gets up to shake her hand.*
FOREIGN SECRETARY: Mrs Paige, we're delighted to see
    you.
CLARA: Sir Robert.
FOREIGN SECRETARY: We've heard of the good work you've
    been doing in Europe.
    (CLARA *smiles.*)
    We need help with the French. To go to Paris to haggle
    about farm prices.
CLARA: I thought Sir Michael was in charge.
FOREIGN SECRETARY: Sir Michael has broken his neck. Out
    riding.
CLARA: Oh Lord. I hope he's all right.
FOREIGN SECRETARY: He's fine. But he's not up to
    haggling. Particularly with the French. Which involves a
    great deal of shaking your head.

I

(The FOREIGN SECRETARY *is already ushering her to the door, the interview over.)*

Good, thank you. Thank you for coming.

CLARA: Not at all.

(The YOUNG MAN *has taken her by the arm to guide her out.)*

FOREIGN SECRETARY: You'll be briefed. *(Nods at the* YOUNG MAN.*)* Arthur.

YOUNG MAN: *(Gestures her through the door)* This way.

INT. FLAT. DAY

CLARA *draws back the big velvet curtain of the sitting room. The man's body is still sprawled on the floor. We see the room is conservatively decorated, heavy with gilt and thick fabrics. She looks down at the body. She goes out to the bathroom and we hear the sound of water being turned on. It runs. Then she returns and drags the body away down the corridor as if it were a corpse.*

INT. FLAT: BEDROOM. DAY

CLARA *is changing. She has just put on a pleated suit. The man appears at the bathroom door. He still has his suit on but it is stained from the shoulders down to the ribcage by the water he has just had poured over his head. He is rubbing himself with a towel. He is* GERALD, *older than she, dry, pawky.*

GERALD: I thought you were in Strasburg.

CLARA: No.

GERALD: Isn't it Thursday?

CLARA: Yes. But it's not the right week.

(He makes a small move of reconciliation towards her.)

No.

(She looks at him from across the room.)

I hate you. You don't believe it. Every time I say it you think it's because of something you've done. The latest incident, whatever it is. You think when the incident's over, oh well, the hatred will be over. But it won't. It's you that I hate. What you are. What you represent. Drink and cowardice in equal parts. The whole dreary mixture disgusts me.

(*There's a pause.*)
You'd better get going. You're late for the House.

EXT. SOUTHALL. NIGHT
*The centre of Southall. It is completely foreign. Indian youths
standing about on street corners, in front of cinemas showing
Hindi films. A street market selling exclusively Indian goods and
food. Women promenading in saris in front of all-night
supermarkets, garishly lit. Everyone in good spirits, laughing and
joking in the streets.
A taxi moving along.* CLARA's *face as she peers anxiously out
from her taxi searching for her destination. As her taxi draws up,
children rush up to sell her nuts from their stalls. Then the taxi
accelerates away.*

EXT. SOUTHALL HALL. NIGHT
*A church hall, surrounded by glistening tarmac. Light shines from
inside. The* SIKH LEADER, *in his fifties with glasses, stands
waiting as* CLARA *hurries from her cab.*
SIKH LEADER: Oh, thank goodness, we were worried.
CLARA: My taxi didn't know where it was.
SIKH LEADER: They never do. Come on in.

INT. SOUTHALL HALL. NIGHT
*Inside the hall there is a gathering of about sixty people,
predominantly Asian, but not entirely. At one end* CLARA *is
standing with a group of eight men, most of them Sikhs, including
the* SIKH LEADER, *to whom she has just presented scrolls.*
CLARA: It's an honour for me to present these community
    awards to these fine men who've done so much to help
    so many newcomers to fit into the host community.
    (*She smiles. The group of eight beam, their scrolls in front of
    them.*)

INT. SOUTHALL HALL. NIGHT
*Later. Question and answer. The chairs have now been ranged in
a circle for an informal session in the middle of the hall. Wives,
children, cakes, cups of tea, old-age pensioners.* CLARA *sitting
forward, listening intently.*

3

SIKH LEADER: But you see, Mrs Paige, we know you are
 sincere . . .
CLARA: Yes . . .
SIKH LEADER: Although your politics are not ours, we know
 you work hard as our European MP. But we are not sure
 what the Common Market does for people like us.
CLARA: Yes, I can see . . .
 (*She nods at a* MOTHER *whose child is about to fall off its
 chair.*)
 I'm sorry, your child is falling off there . . .
MOTHER: Oh, thank you . . .
CLARA: Yes, you may think what's this parliament miles
 away in Strasburg got to do with me, how does it
 actually affect my daily life . . .
SIKH LEADER: That's right.
CLARA: But you see it is the embodiment of an ideal. Peace
 and prosperity in Europe. And these are things in which
 we will all believe.
 (*She looks round.*)

INT. SOUTHALL HALL. NIGHT
The meeting over, most people have gone. The SIKH LEADER *is*

glowing with the success of it. A few stragglers behind them, as they head for the entranceway.

SIKH LEADER: We're all pleased to have such a star represent us.

CLARA: Well, thank you.

SIKH LEADER: Let me find you a car.

(*He goes.* CLARA *stands alone just inside the entrance. She looks round. She is suddenly aware there is nobody about. She looks to the window by the entrance. Outside a man is standing alone under a lamp-post. The tarmac is glistening below him. He has a weak, pallid face, crinkly black hair. He is in his forties. He is standing in the rain, waiting patiently in a mackintosh. We see him through the window. Then we see the look on* CLARA's *face. Then the* SIKH LEADER *returns.*)

CLARA: Excuse me . . . I wonder . . . it's just . . . there's someone out there. Do you think I might go out the back way?

INT. SOUTHALL HALL. NIGHT
From above we see the SIKH LEADER *lead* CLARA *fast through the darkened and deserted hall to a back exit.*

EXT. SOUTHALL ALLEYWAY. NIGHT
They come fast down a filthy alleyway, loaded with crates and orange boxes, at the back of the hall. It has high walls on either side. They come to the end of the alleyway. A deserted street.

CLARA: Well, thank you.

(*She shakes his hand.*)
Goodnight.

INT. FLAT: BEDROOM. NIGHT
CLARA's *in bed, asleep. The moon beyond her window. The curtain moving in the breeze. The telephone rings beside the bed. She wakes up. We are very close. She reaches for it.*

CLARA: Yes?

VOICE: I know what you're doing. (*A pause.*) I know who you are.

(CLARA *does not answer.*)

5

Where's your husband? He isn't with you. Where is he?
(*She turns. The bed is indeed empty beside her.*)
Why don't you ask *me* to come round?
(*She pauses a second, then puts the phone down. She sits up, frightened. After a few moments, the sound of the latch-key in the door. She looks through the open bedroom door to the front door.* GERALD *stands in coat and hat, a black figure silhouetted. Strong light from the corridor behind him.*)
CLARA: God, you scared me.
GERALD: I have no idea what you mean.

EXT. PAULINE'S HOUSE. DAY
CLARA *getting out of her BMW outside a house in Hampstead. She hurries through, followed by her secretary* SANDRA, *a young woman in her twenties in jeans and a sweater. At the back of the house is a garden where* PAULINE, *who is about thirty, is sitting in a deckchair, shelling peas. The garden is idyllically green and pleasant.*
CLARA: Oh, Pauline, my goodness, I'm sorry . . .
PAULINE: Calm down, it's all right.
CLARA: I'm *sorry.*
PAULINE: Calm down. He's fine. Aren't you?
(*She turns her head. Out of the bushes has appeared a thin, fair-haired boy of eight.* CLARA *kneels on the grass to embrace* SIMON.)
CLARA: My darling, how are you? I was going to come yesterday and I just got so busy.
PAULINE: He's been fine.
SIMON: Hello, Mum.
CLARA: Did you miss me? I'm sorry. The worst is over, I promise you that.
(SANDRA *watches from a discreet distance,* CLARA *still on her knees, getting out a box of chocolates.*)
Here, look, they're from Fortnums, the gooey ones you like . . .
(*As she speaks a clockwork train goes by them on a track that leads right the way round the garden.*)
What's this ? Did you make this?
SIMON: Well, mostly.

PAULINE: Would you like a cup of tea?

CLARA: Yes, please.

SIMON: I'll show you . . .

(*But* CLARA *has already begun to walk with* PAULINE *towards the patio.*)

CLARA: It's just been hectic. With all this enabling legislation. It has to be taken through point by point. They just dumped it in my lap and said, 'Look, use the summer recess to go through it.'

PAULINE: Well, it's nice to be needed.

CLARA: Yes. It isn't all bad.

(*They have reached a garden table where a teapot is waiting, and cups.* CLARA *looks down the garden to where* SIMON *is playing with* SANDRA, *a little boy in a very big garden.*)

What about you? You've had your hair cut. It looks so

attractive.

PAULINE: Clara, I'm your sister. It's a perfectly ordinary haircut. Neither good nor bad. (*She smiles.*) I don't need flattery. You *have* my vote.

INT. CLARA'S CAR. DAY
Back in the BMW, travelling fast along the North Circular.
SANDRA *is in the passenger seat, reading from a huge diary on her knees in front of her. It is balanced on top of a pile of correspondence and files.* SIMON *is sitting silently in the back.*
SANDRA: The Minister at four to discuss new European legislation. There's a drinks party for the Road Transport Lobby at six.
CLARA: Uh-huh.
SANDRA: Can you see the diary?
    (*She holds it on her knee so* CLARA *can drive and snatch glances at it at the same time.*)
    Also . . .
CLARA: (*Catching her tone*) Yes?
SANDRA: A man's been calling the office. He says he's a friend of yours. His name is . . .
    (CLARA *interrupts, changing gear.*)
CLARA: If it's who I think it is, the answer is no.

INT. FLAT: KITCHEN. DAY
SIMON *is now seated on the counter in Clara's kitchen. She is in the bedroom, packing a case as she calls through to him.*
CLARA: So did you have a nice time at Pauline's?
SIMON: No.
CLARA: I know you did. You always do. You always say you prefer it to home.
    (*She comes into the kitchen, passing him to go to the airing cupboard and get clothes.* SANDRA *is stacking papers in another corner of the kitchen.*)
SANDRA: Do you want these?
CLARA: Yes, I do. Oh, Sandra, the stuff about education . . .
    (CLARA *turns back to* SIMON *as* SANDRA *returns to the papers.*)
    And how was school?

9

SIMON: Horrible.

CLARA: Simon, you do make me laugh.

> (*The doorbell goes. She passes again, on her way to answer, as* GERALD *appears in the kitchen doorway, with a small bag, in his coat.*)

GERALD: (*To Simon*) Sorry, old chap . . .

CLARA: (*Passing him*) I'll get it.

GERALD: Got to spend the weekend at my constituency. Listening to a lot of people moan.

> (*He reaches down and kisses the boy. As he does so we can hear* CLARA *greeting* DELIA *outside.*)

DELIA: Clara, how are you?

CLARA: I'm fine.

DELIA: You look wonderful.

CLARA: What a nice haircut.

DELIA: Oh, good.

CLARA: Come on through.

> (*They come through the kitchen door.* DELIA *is in her thirties, with three children, the very spirit of middle-class motherhood.*)

Here we are. Look, here's Delia.

> (DELIA *goes across to greet* SIMON. *Children, far too small for* SIMON, *are dumped on the counter beside him.*)

DELIA: Here are all your friends.

CLARA: Excuse me.

> (CLARA *leaves the kitchen and walks down the corridor to where* GERALD *is putting on his coat.*)

I'm sorry.

GERALD: No.

CLARA: About yesterday. I went too far.

> (*He just looks at her. At the far end of the corridor a* MINICAB DRIVER *has appeared at the open door.*)

MINICAB DRIVER: Car for Mr Paige.

GERALD: Yes, I'm coming.

CLARA: If we just had some time.

> (*He looks at her a moment, as if considering this, but not thinking it true.* SANDRA *pops out of the kitchen and calls down the corridor.*)

SANDRA: Your car's here.

(GERALD *heads off down the hall.* CLARA *goes back into the kitchen, and approaches* SIMON.)

CLARA: Now good – you lucky boy – I'm going to miss you. But anyway. Here. Give your mother a kiss.
(SIMON *leans forward and presses his cheek close to hers. She is smiling. He is not. We are very close.*)

INT. COUNTRY HOUSE. DAY
We are behind CLARA *again as she now hurries into the hall of a fine Georgian house in the country. From the hall you would not know if it were public or private. It is grand and spacious. Only a small table set up in the hall and the presence of some security men betray its real function.* CLARA *runs into* JACK SIDMOUTH *who is coming from another direction. He is tall, thin, in his mid-fifties, with greased-down hair and a very county manner of dressing and speaking.*

SIDMOUTH: You're a bit late.

CLARA: I know. I had to give out some community awards.

SIDMOUTH: My God. You do take it seriously. Meeting the people.

CLARA: Isn't that meant to be part of the job?
(SIDMOUTH *smiles. The room in front of them is large and ornate, a sitting room with hard and soft chairs ranged round informally with about twenty-five people in them. They are listening to an* ENGLISH LECTURER *at the far end. Before she can go in, an arm is put around her by* ADAM GILLVRAY. *He is in his forties, with a boxer's face and silvery hair. He is technically not very good-looking, but there is a dynamism that makes him attractive; or, rather, confident of his own attractiveness.*)

GILLVRAY: Clara, we'd given up hope of you.

CLARA: Adam. They tell me you're today's star.

GILLVRAY: Me the star? No. Aren't you? Don't we see you everywhere?
(CLARA *has begun talking on top of him already, and in addition they have been joined from the room by* LADY BOEING, *the organizer of the event. A handsome woman in her fifties, with elaborate coiffure. Now all three of them are speaking at once.*)

11

CLARA: Me? Not really.

LADY BOEING: Hello, Clara, my dear, how are you? This came for you.

(*She hands* CLARA *an envelope. On it, in big writing, very neat, the words* 'CLARA PAIGE'. *She opens it while the chatter goes on.*)

GILLVRAY: Television, radio, it seems to be you on every channel.

LADY BOEING: From a man in a blue blazer. And he sweated a lot.

CLARA: Adam's exaggerating.

GILLVRAY: Only a little. Still, I suppose if there has to be a new wave, it's best it looks like you.

(CLARA *is reading the note, alarmed, distracted. We see the words: 'vital we meet'. She looks up. A silence.* GILLVRAY *is smiling.*)

CLARA: What? Oh yes.

(*Now a number of heads in the room have turned to see who's at the door. For the first time we are conscious of the* ENGLISH LECTURER's *voice in the background.*)

ENGLISH LECTURER: In Hobbes's *Leviathan*, we find the classic text of seventeenth-century conservatism . . .

(CLARA *looks to* GILLVRAY.)

CLARA: Hadn't we better sit down?

EXT. COUNTRY HOUSE. EVENING
The house seen from outside at night. Inside the drawing room, people are standing about with drinks. Out of a side door, CLARA *appears and slips away quietly across a lawn. In the back garden, she disappears down towards a lake.*

EXT. COUNTRY TOWN. EVENING
A small country town in the late evening. Nothing moves. A cross in the middle of a deserted road. The shops all shut. The only lit building The George, an enormous old hotel, more like a stableyard than a pub. CLARA *hurrying across the deserted road. She comes to a cattle market. She threads her way through dozens of metal cattle pens. At the centre of the market, standing outside a colonnaded building is* MICHAEL SWANTON. *He is alone,*

sweating slightly in a blue blazer and grey flannels and with a regimental tie. His coat is folded over his arm. We recognize him as the man who stood under the lamp-post.

SWANTON: Hello, Clara.

CLARA: Michael.

SWANTON: It's nice to see you. It's been a long time.

(*She passes him and goes inside the central building.*)

INT. AUCTION HOUSE. EVENING

CLARA *comes in to the auction area which has a high cupola through which shafts of evening light fall.* SWANTON *follows.*

SWANTON: You're getting very big.

CLARA: Nobody's big in England. (*She sits, smiling, still wary.*) So you'd better tell me, what do you want?

SWANTON: Well, I heard the Jack Absalom Society was having a weekend – what is it, by the way?

CLARA: A conservative philosophy group.

SWANTON: High-powered, plainly.

CLARA: Old friends, that's all. Taking time off, Michael, from busy schedules to discuss some of the philosophical issues.

SWANTON: Yes.

(*He is still standing. There is an edge in both their manners.*) To be frank, the only reason I'm here is because I read about your group in the paper. I wanted to talk to you.

CLARA: Talk to me?

SWANTON: Only business, that's all.

CLARA: (*At once, alarmed*) Oh, look now, Michael, please . . .

SWANTON: No, listen . . .

CLARA: Come on.

SWANTON: Just hear me out. It's nothing like last time.

CLARA: Michael, I have this fear of prison. Is that unreasonable? For a Member of the European Parliament?

SWANTON: There's no question of that. (*He is suddenly firm.*) I have a scheme. In the field of microchip technology. I could explain. But I think it would go over your head. In some ways it goes over mine. *But* . . . (*He pauses, confident.*) The result would be an all-British wrist-watch which is also a television as well.

13

(CLARA *looks at him uncharitably.*)

CLARA: Michael, do you know how much capital investment . . .

SWANTON: (*Speaking over her*) Of course . . .

CLARA: . . . is needed for microchip work?

SWANTON: (*Over her again*) For production. Not for research. For research you just need a bloke – which I have – a friend of mine, who's a genius. You'd like him. Honestly. In Wales you can pick up these government grants. From Gerald and you I'd want less than a quarter. Eighty thousand at most. (*He is suddenly quiet.*) And in return you wouldn't hear from me. Until I repaid you, of course.

(CLARA *stands, uncharmed.*)

CLARA: Is there a prospectus?

SWANTON: A what?

CLARA: A prospectus. Have you written out a specification for the project?

SWANTON: Oh, really, would you think . . . do you really need that? Given what you know of me? Or to put it more directly . . .

CLARA: Yes?

SWANTON: What I know of you.

(*He looks down, sheepish at saying this, as if he wanted to be nice.*)

CLARA: Say, 'I know who you are.'

SWANTON: What?

CLARA: Just say it.

(SWANTON *looks puzzled.*)

Have you rung my flat?

SWANTON: I wouldn't dream of ringing you. What? You mean without saying who I was?

CLARA: All right, yes, I'm sorry. (*She gets up to leave.*) It was a mistake.

SWANTON: Clara. My money.

(*She turns and looks back at him.*)

CLARA: Give me a few days. I need time to think.

INT. COUNTRY HOUSE: DINING ROOM. NIGHT
*An oval table with candles and silver. Twenty people in all. All
in dinner dress. Crystal glasses, three kinds each. Everyone is
being served Beef Wellington.* GILLVRAY *is staring at* CLARA,
as if waiting. Finally she relents and speaks to him.
CLARA: So. I'm only sorry your wife couldn't make it.
GILLVRAY: Weren't you two at school?
CLARA: We were.
GILLVRAY: Did you hear? She's having another baby.
    (*All the diners smile, as if this were a well-known joke.*)
CLARA: Goodness, but don't you have . . .
GILLVRAY: Six. Now we're going to have seven. I believe in
    practising what I preach. After all, my book on the
    family . . .
CLARA: I'm hoping to get time to read it.
GILLVRAY: The basic conservative unit, am I right?
CLARA: Well, certainly you seem to think so.
    (*They smile.*)
    When's the baby due?
GILLVRAY: Oh, any time. In fact very probably tonight. (*He
    laughs and reaches into his pocket to display a bleeper.*)
    Look here, this way I can go for a walk. If it bleeps,
    then I know it's coming. Or of course it may be the PM.
    One or the other.
CLARA: I see. But where is she bleeping from?
GILLVRAY: Angela? Oh, I leave her at home.

INT. COUNTRY HOUSE: DINING ROOM. NIGHT
Later. Port and nuts. The débris of a good meal. GILLVRAY
now holding forth to the whole table.
GILLVRAY: Oh, yes, I do think people finally *know*. I mean,
    most people know what to do. Their gut instinct tells
    them. If you listen to that . . . well, in my view, you
    can't go far wrong. (*He smiles at* CLARA.) I mean I can
    remember when I was a Socialist . . .
    (*Mixed laughter round the table.*)
    All right, but a lot of historians were . . . then there was
    always this agony. '*Should* I do this?' 'Oooh, I wonder,
    is this right? Is this wrong?' Then when I saw the light,

15

I do remember this weight being lifted. No more having
to think. Not wasting your life in uncertainty and guilt.
Do what you want to. Surely?
(*He looks around.* CLARA *is affected by this speech,
thoughtful, as if making up her mind. A* MAN *bangs the
table gently.*)
MAN: Hear. Hear.
GILLVRAY: That's the basis of freedom. At this table . . .
surely . . . that's what everyone wants?
(*He challenges anyone to refute him with his look.* CLARA
looks down, decisive now.)

INT. COUNTRY HOUSE: DRAWING ROOM. NIGHT
They have all come out of the dining room, and SIDMOUTH *is
reaching across* CLARA *to get himself some coffee from a silver
tray in the yellow satin drawing room.* CLARA *is in a deep
armchair with a calvados.*
SIDMOUTH: Well, of course, he's an absolute wanker.
    Converts are always the worst, don't you think?
CLARA: (*Smiles*) I suppose.
    (SIDMOUTH *sits down next to her.*)
SIDMOUTH: I mean, you were brought up in the faith.
    Where were you?
CLARA: Birmingham.
SIDMOUTH: Good. But these ghastly intellectuals the PM's
    taken up with, I mean, it's just fancy dressing, isn't it?
    (CLARA *frowns slightly.*)
CLARA: Fancy dressing for what?
SIDMOUTH: Well, I would think for power.
CLARA: And is this fancy dressing? This whole occasion?
SIDMOUTH: It's not disco dancing, is it, my dear?

INT. COUNTRY HOUSE: CLARA'S BEDROOM. NIGHT
A fine bed. Simple light furnishings in the grand Georgian room.

The bedside lamp already on, casting a warm light. A door to the bathroom open and lit. CLARA *is sitting fully clothed on the side of her bed, phone in hand. We move in towards her. A voice at the other end is heard to say, 'Hello'.*

CLARA: I've decided no, that's the end of it.

SWANTON'S VOICE: Clara?

CLARA: Absolutely not. I won't pay. What happened this evening was blackmail . . . (*She prevents him interrupting.*) . . . please let me finish . . . because you think you can bring up my past and ruin my career. But I promise you . . . you have no such power. Michael, I'm calling your bluff.

(*She puts the phone down before he can answer. The moment it hits the cradle, it begins to ring again. She looks at it, alarmed. Then very cautiously she lifts it.*)

VOICE: You don't fancy a nightcap?

CLARA: Who's that?

VOICE: It's a well-known Conservative philosopher.

CLARA: Oh, Adam, I'm already in bed.

(*There is a long pause while they both work this out.*)

GILLVRAY'S VOICE: Fine. Goodnight.

CLARA: Goodnight.

(*She puts the phone down. Then she turns to the heap of files that are in her attaché case by the bed. She throws them down to prepare for a night's work. The camera travels towards her as she puts on her glasses. We move further in. Then just as we are over her, we move off her and up away towards the wall.*)

EXT. COUNTRY HOUSE. DAY

A fine morning. The formal drive to the house. A Mini Metro, looking rather absurd, heads towards the house.

INT. COUNTRY HOUSE: DRAWING ROOM. DAY

The light now pouring through the windows of the drawing room. The whole study group is ranged about in chairs, informally, being lectured by a man with a foreign accent who has long hair and who keeps referring to economic charts on his blackboard.

FOREIGN LECTURER: Let's look at the philosophy of the

National Health Service, which up till now has been regarded as one of our – er – English success stories but which we're coming to realize in fact could be much more efficient, much more answerable to the public's needs were it to be – er privately run.

(CLARA *is sitting staring straight ahead into the distance.* GILLVRAY *is behind her ostentatiously reading the Sunday paper.* CLARA *notices the Mini Metro before it disappears from view. She looks round to see if anyone else has noticed. No one has. Then suddenly* SWANTON's *face appears at the window behind the* FOREIGN LECTURER. *He waves at her for a second, before being yanked violently away by two huge security men with walkie-talkies.* CLARA *looks round. No one else has noticed. Then she gets up.*)

INT. COUNTRY HOUSE: HALL. DAY
CLARA *comes quickly into the empty hall where only the organizer of the event,* LADY BOEING, *is sitting at her little desk. She goes to the open door of the house. There,* SWANTON *is seen arguing with two security men. As soon as she sees them,* CLARA *steps back behind a pillar to avoid being seen, but as she does,* SWANTON *lifts his arm and points straight at her.*
SWANTON: That's her.

INT. COUNTRY HOUSE: HALL. DAY
People are now gathering in groups to talk in the hall informally, a few with pre-lunchtime drinks, as the session breaks up in the drawing room. CLARA *is arguing furiously with* SWANTON *in one corner of the hall.* SWANTON *looks out of place in an attempt at country clothes – check jacket and flannels with an old mac on top.*
CLARA: How dare you come here? Look around you. Do you have no idea who these people are? (*She smiles at a couple of distinguished old men as they walk by.*) I'm trying to keep everything together. I am working fourteen hours a day, I have a family as well . . .
SWANTON: I just need money. Clara, you're my last chance. I am begging you.
(*He looks at her. You think she is about to give in, but*

instead she walks away to the security men.)
CLARA: (*Quietly*) Please. Mr Swanton is ready to leave.
(*She looks down.*)

INT. HOTEL. DAY
The CONCIERGE *of a big Right Bank hotel in Paris is holding a
telephone call. Beyond him, ranks of keys and messages. A
marble desk with low lighting. At once he nods at* CLARA, *who is
standing dressed as we last saw her, by the desk.*
CONCIERGE: Vous avez votre numéro, madame.
(*He nods at the small wooden booth towards which* CLARA
now heads to pick up the receiver.)
CLARA: Gerald. Gerald. It's Clara.
(GERALD'*s voice is muzzy and distorted.*)
GERALD'S VOICE: Hello.
CLARA: You're back. Have I woken you? Look, I've had to
go sooner than I thought. I went straight to the airport.
GERALD'S VOICE: Why?
CLARA: I'll tell you why later, I just had to get out.
GERALD'S VOICE: Get out?
CLARA: The thing is . . . it's just I promised Simon I'd call
by Pauline's tonight and read him a story. If you could
go.
GERALD'S VOICE: It's always me.
(*A pause.*)
CLARA: Well, if you can, will you? I'd be really grateful.
GERALD'S VOICE: I'll do it.
CLARA: That's really sweet of you. Thanks.
(*She says it kindly. Then she puts the phone down, without
a goodbye. She stands a moment, as if a great weight has
been lifted. Free at last. With a smile she goes to the desk,
picks up her key and her baggage, and walks towards the
elevator. As she does she passes a group of men in suits who
are standing talking in French. As she waits for the elevator
one of them has come towards her. In his thirties, he has a
calm manner, which suggests a practical bent. He also has a
faint air of amusement, which is charming.* CLARA *smiles at
him instinctively. His name is* WALLACE SHARP.)
WALLACE: Hello, is it – Clara Paige, isn't it?

CLARA: That's right. Hello.
  (*There's a slight pause.*)
  I smile at everyone. It's a habit. It's safest for a
  politician.
WALLACE: You have no reason to remember but I'm Wallace
  Sharp.
CLARA: Yes, of course.
WALLACE: You helped me with the siting of a factory in
  France.
CLARA: How is it?
WALLACE: We're about to sell two thousand bedside lights to
  a chain of French motels.
CLARA: Is that what you do? I can't remember.
WALLACE: Yes. I design.

CLARA: Well, that's excellent. That you sold so many.
   (WALLACE *shrugs.*)
WALLACE: In a way.
CLARA: What do you mean?
WALLACE: I'm bored already. I'm thinking of the next thing.
   I never stick at anything for long. (*He is looking her
   straight in the eye. Then he turns to the men who are waiting
   a few paces off.*) Un moment. Je viens. (*He turns back to
   CLARA.*) Would you like a drink?
CLARA: A drink? Would I like a drink? Gosh. I mean, well, I
   mean, goodness. No, I couldn't possibly. Hold on, no,
   yes, I would.

INT. HOTEL: BAR. DAY
*The tiny bar of the hotel. It is rose-coloured, exquisite, deserted.
Behind them are dioramas of eighteenth-century life in France.
There are hand-painted murals behind a simple bar. Roses at the
little dark tables.* CLARA *is on a banquette as* WALLACE
approaches with a BARMAN.
WALLACE: What would you like?
CLARA: I don't know. I can't think. What do people have?
   (*She laughs.*) I'm sorry, no, I'm being silly. Gin and
   vermouth.
WALLACE: Deux, s'il vous plaît. (*The* BARMAN *goes.*)
   You seem rather light-headed.
CLARA: I was glad to get out of England, that's all.
WALLACE: Are you often in Paris?
CLARA: No. Sadly. The parliament moves between
   Luxemburg and Strasburg. Both very boring towns. But
   I was brought up in Birmingham, so it's fine.
   (*They smile.*)
WALLACE: Is your husband with you?
CLARA: Gerald? No, Gerald's too busy – it's a shame.
   (*The* BARMAN *sets down two Martinis.*)
   What about you?
WALLACE: Me?
CLARA: Yes.
WALLACE: Oh, I don't really live anywhere, if that's what
   you mean. It's all a question of where I can work. My

22

sister is married to a Frenchman. So when I'm in Paris,
I stay in their flat.
CLARA: I love being abroad. I feel safe. It's like aeroplanes.
From the moment you get on, till the moment you
leave, no one can get at you.
WALLACE: I have.
CLARA: Yes. But you don't want anything. So you don't
count.
(*Before she can reach for her drink, a tall, middle-aged
Englishman in a suit has appeared with a sidekick, seeking
her out. He is called* SLATE-ESCOTT.)
SLATE-ESCOTT: Ah, there you are. We heard you'd arrived
early . . .

(*She gets up at once, the two drinks untouched in front of them.*)

CLARA: Yes.

SLATE-ESCOTT: If we'd known we'd have sent you a car.

WALLACE: If you have any time, I know Paris very well.

(*He has not got up. She has picked up her handbag from the banquette beside her.*)

CLARA: Yes, call me.

(*She turns and smiles at* WALLACE. SLATE-ESCOTT *gives* WALLACE *a filthy look, as if this young man has no right to be with* CLARA. *Then* CLARA *turns and follows him.*)

SLATE-ESCOTT: We have all the relevant briefing documents. We're waiting to see which way the Germans will jump.

CLARA: Ah, yes.

SLATE-ESCOTT: They like to keep their cards pretty close to their chest. I suppose you might say, who can blame them? (WALLACE *watches as they disappear up the stairs, not turning towards him.*)

INT. HOTEL. DAY

CLARA *and* SLATE-ESCOTT *continue up the stairs,* SLATE-ESCOTT *talking all the time.*

SLATE-ESCOTT: The Dutch, I suppose they're pretty dependable, the Spaniards pretty good. At least they have been in the past. As for the Belgians, well, I have never met a Belgian who didn't understand the basics. (CLARA *stops suddenly. She puts her hand on* SLATE-ESCOTT'*s wrist. He stops and looks at her.*)

CLARA: I am sorry. There's something I forgot to say to my friend.

INT. ZINYAFSKIS' APARTMENT: KITCHEN. NIGHT

The kitchen of the Zinyafskis' apartment, which gives out on to their dining room. The kitchen itself is small and narrow, with an enamel stove and a very heavy old-fashioned white sink. Saucepans hang around the walls. MADAME ZINYAFSKI *is cooking pot-au-feu for the first course. She is tasting her sauce. She is a woman, probably in her late sixties, very dark indeed, and big.*

MADAME ZINYAFSKI: Ah, ça va, ce sera excellent.
(Her daughter-in-law, VIOLET, *is standing beside her, busy helping.* VIOLET *is in her late twenties, a sensible girl, thin and relaxed. She is trying to persuade* MADAME ZINYAFSKI *to add wine.)*
Ah, non, non, non, n'ajoute pas ça. C'est toujours tellement acide. Si tu veux, tu peux couper le persil là-bas.
*(*VIOLET *turns smiling at* WALLACE *and* CLARA *who are standing by the high glass doors of the kitchen, watching.* VIOLET *passes through them to the narrow dining room which has very little decoration but for an exquisitely polished floor and a big gilt mirror.* WALLACE *is smiling.)*
WALLACE: Look, you see, Violet's mother-in-law is the best Yiddish French cook in Paris.
*(*WALLACE *has put his arms round his sister's mother-in-law and is kissing the back of her neck, rather impishly.)*
MADAME ZINYAFSKI: Ah, ce n'est pas vrai.
WALLACE: Gefilte coq au vin, that's her speciality.
*(*VIOLET, *who has come back to taste the pot-au-feu, smiles.)*
MADAME ZINYAFSKI: *(To* CLARA*)* Vous voyez . . .
VIOLET: Ah, maman, c'est vraiment delicieux.
MADAME ZINYAFSKI: He is insolent.
CLARA: Very.
(Behind her two children have now appeared in white nightdresses and beyond them the men have arrived to sit down for their dinner. There is HECTOR, *Violet's husband, who is in a red check shirt, a very big, tough man in his twenties reading the paper. And his brother, who is in his early twenties with a beard and a skullcap. He is tucking his napkin into his collar. Violet's children are jumping up and down.)*
CHILDREN: Maman, maman, nous voulons manger avec vous ce soir.
MADAME ZINYAFSKI: Non, c'est impossible.
VIOLET: Vous avez déjà mangé.
*(*CLARA *is watching them as they move over, jumping and pulling at their grandmother's skirt, begging her to let them*

stay up.)

WALLACE: You have children?

CLARA: I have a son.

INT. ZINYAFSKIS' APARTMENT: DINING ROOM. NIGHT
Later. MADAME ZINYAFSKI *moves round the big long dining table dishing out pot-au-feu with an enormous spoon from a big black pot into soup plates. Everyone is sitting at table, all talking at once, their napkins tucked in, their bits of bread pocked with nibbling at their sides. They are all talking at once, smiling, arguing.* CLARA *watches for the first time in the film relaxed, off guard. She catches* WALLACE's *eye across the table and smiles.*

INT. ZINYAFSKIS' APARTMENT: DINING ROOM. NIGHT
Later. They are sitting round, but the conversation has now focused down to PAUL *and* HECTOR *who are in mid-speech. They are all grounded contentedly after the pot-au-feu. But* PAUL *is serious.*

HECTOR: Je suis français, Paul, et fous-moi la paix avec tes histoires d'être juif ou pas.

PAUL: A une époque en France, on a appris aux gens à connaître les juifs, et moi, j'ai le sentiment aujourd'hui que ces gens là, leurs enfants, reconnaissent d'abord le juif en toi, pas le français.

MADAME ZINYAFSKI: Mais, ça fait deux mille ans que ça dure.

HECTOR: Deux mille ans, deux mille ans, on est en quatre-vingt sept. Arrête, Paul, c'est fini ces histoires.

WALLACE: Are you getting this?

CLARA: Pretty well. Being Jewish means being aware of history.

WALLACE: Paul feels a Jew is always going to be a stranger in any country.

CLARA: Oui, je comprends cela.

(*And suddenly* CLARA *is animatedly joining in the debate. Everyone at the table now starts putting their point of view,* PAUL *arguing that the Jews can never truly belong,* HECTOR *arguing the opposite,* CLARA *interspersing questions in French. It is plain she catches every nuance of the*

*conversation. One of the children appears meanwhile and
slips silently on to* HECTOR's *lap. He draws her to his chest
without even noticing.*)

PAUL: On ne sera jamais intégré. On est toujours des invités.

HECTOR: Tout ça n'est plus vrai, plus maintenant. Tout a
changé. Comment on dit en anglais? 'Nous sommes
intégrés.'

(WALLACE *smiles at* CLARA.)

WALLACE: 'We belong.'

EXT. STREET. NIGHT

CLARA *and* WALLACE *walking together down the tiny rue des
Rosiers. It is dark, but each shop they pass is like a tiny cave
with a light burning inside it, and shelves stacked with odd goods.
It is all so poky and intricate that the feeling is more like North
Africa than Paris. They stop for a moment to watch an incredibly
old woman have pulses weighed out for her on some primitive
scales.*

CLARA: Look . . .

WALLACE: Yes, I know. It's extraordinary. The Marais
doesn't change. The rest of Paris is ruined. Well, it is,
isn't it? It's all art galleries and banks. This is the last bit
of what you could actually call Paris. And even this is
going very fast.

EXT. CAFÉ MAISON COLLIN. NIGHT

*A 'fin-de-siècle' café in the Marais. They sit at ease drinking
black coffee and calvados. Mirrors behind them reflect the zinc-
topped bar and the regulars who all stand.* WALLACE *is looking
at* CLARA, CLARA *is dreaming, looking ahead.* WALLACE *has
picked up a paper napkin and is sketching on it.*

WALLACE: So you were always going to be in politics?

CLARA: No. I was in business. When my mother died she left
me a couple of houses. Property. Which I rented out.
Then Gerald came along – with a partner of his – and
suggested we start a mail-order business. (*She smiles at
him, a little blank.*) That was fine for a while.

WALLACE: The business crashed?

CLARA: Not exactly. There was a tight patch in the late

seventies. We'd over-expanded. We had to hive off the loss-making parts. The dress side got some bad publicity, people who sent cheques for goods they never received, but by then it was no longer ours. Legally.

WALLACE: Who owned it?

CLARA: The partner. He was called Swanton.

WALLACE: Swanton?

CLARA: Michael Swanton.

(WALLACE *is looking at her, an unspoken question in the air.*)

Oh, a rather sad man.

(*She looks down at his drawing.* WALLACE *has drawn her. She looks romantic, a little haunted, tender.*)

CLARA: I don't look like that.

WALLACE: Yes you do. To me. Don't you see it?

(*She puts her hand on it and moves it across the table towards her.*)

CLARA: Yes. I do now.

EXT. PARIS SQUARE. NIGHT

They come out of the rue des Rosiers into the small square at its end. A few kosher grocery shops but otherwise neat and quiet, almost provincial. CLARA *looks at the deserted square.*

CLARA: How I envy you this. This easiness.

WALLACE: Yes. It's fresh air.

(*They look a moment at a plaque on the school wall:* 165 ENFANTS JUIFS DE CETTE ÉCOLE DÉPORTÉS EN ALLEMAGNE DURANT LA SECONDE GUERRE MONDIALE FURENT EXTERMINÉS DANS LES CAMPS NAZIS. N'OUBLIEZ PAS.)

'A hundred and sixty-five Jewish children from this school deported to Germany during the Second World War were exterminated in Nazi camps. Never forget.'

(CLARA *looks down a moment. In the silent square,* WALLACE *reaches across and kisses her cheek. She smiles at him, then looks away.*)

CLARA: I have a fantasy now. I shall walk round Paris all night. And when dawn comes, I shall be sitting under the Eiffel Tower to watch it. And then I shall have to go back to work.

(WALLACE *smiles*.)

Thank you for the most wonderful night.

(*She backs a couple of paces, and then turns to go.*)

WALLACE: Do you want me to walk with you?

CLARA: No. Not tonight.

(*She smiles, then he watches her walk away contentedly. At the end of the square, she turns and waves. She's gone. He turns, slightly bewildered by the suddenness of her departure.*)

EXT. PARIS STREET. NIGHT

We are beside CLARA *as she walks along a quiet, dark street. Her heels click hypnotically on the pavement. Suddenly she stops, alarmed. She looks down. A cat has stepped out of the doorway in front of her and is looking at her. She smiles, happy by herself, and walks on.*

EXT. RIGHT BANK. NIGHT

Now through deserted Paris. The big, dark, official buildings beautiful as she passes. The night is now completely still. She crosses the deserted road to look down at the river. Then she takes a few paces and begins to cross the Pont des Arts.

EXT. PONT DES ARTS. NIGHT

We see the bridge from her point of view as she steps on to it. It is a pedestrian bridge, with lights irregular and dim across it. It is apparently deserted. But as CLARA *moves a little further down it, she can see a figure in a raincoat, standing between the lamps so we cannot see his face. Before we know who he is, she stops dead. She looks white, angry. He steps out of the shadow. It is* SWANTON.

SWANTON: Clara!

(*She begins to move towards him.*)

CLARA: What are you doing?

SWANTON: Nothing.

CLARA: What d'you mean?

(*She reaches him, and gives him a little push on the shoulder, not wholly in control.*)

SWANTON: Hey. I'm doing nothing.
>   (*She pushes him again. He falls back a little. Suddenly she says in a passionate whisper.*)
CLARA: You are following me!
>   (*He is against the rail of the bridge. Suddenly on an impulse she reaches down and seizes his knees. She overturns him backwards. He falls silently and without crying into the river below. There is a moment. She looks round. There is nobody on the bridge but away on the river's edge a couple are kissing. They do not turn. CLARA moves across to the other side of the bridge and looks down. Behind her, on the pavement, is lying her bag which has slipped off in the effort. She looks down to the water where SWANTON's body is now moving obscurely downstream, face down, no more than a dark patch on the water. She looks up again as if to see if anyone is aware of this lump. She moves back to the original spot. She is sweating. She looks round again, then she starts to move back the way she has come, towards the Left Bank. Then she turns and goes back in the opposite direction. From nowhere, completely by surprise, a cyclist flashes past her, dangerously close. She jumps. Then she seems relieved, and she begins to walk towards the Right Bank. As she walks, she looks to the kissing couple, who are now closer to her, down on the quai. The man has his eyes closed as he kisses the girl, but now he opens them, and is looking directly at CLARA. He is still kissing. She turns her head and leaves the bridge.*)

EXT. LOUVRE. NIGHT
CLARA *is walking along, beginning to hurry, beside the wall of the Louvre. We come to some arches through which we see two enormous yellow cement containers, lit in the night on a building site, unexpectedly found in the middle of the Louvre.*

EXT. ORANGERIE. NIGHT
CLARA *walking fast along beside the wall on the east side of the Place de la Concorde. We pull out to reveal the Orangerie behind her.*

30

EXT. PALAIS ROYAL. NIGHT

CLARA *begins to run, for no reason quickening her pace, faster and faster, until she is running flat out through the night, and along the arcade by the Palais Royal.*

INT. HOTEL. NIGHT

CLARA *walks up to the desk where the* NIGHT CLERK *is on duty. He is a dark, heavy-browed man in his mid-forties.*

CLARA: Deux cent quarante, s'il vous plaît.

> (*He turns to get the key, running his finger along the line. But it's not there. He turns back.*)

NIGHT CLERK: Vous l'avez déjà, madame.

CLARA: Non, ce n'est pas possible, J'ai . . .

> (*She feels for the bag which ought to be over her shoulder. But it's not there. The* NIGHT CLERK *is staring at her.*) Ah non, j'ai oublié. (*She smiles, flustered.*) Ah oui, je l'en ai. J'ai oublié.
> (*He is just staring at her. Neither of them move. Then she takes a couple of paces backwards, thinking, not really knowing what she's doing.*)

NIGHT CLERK: Can I help you madame?

CLARA: No, no really.

> (*She walks decisively towards the lift, panicking, lost. She turns back. The* NIGHT CLERK *is still watching her. So she goes and hides from him in the small corridor by the telephone booths. She is now out of his sight. She stands there a moment, working out what to do. She moves back towards the corner and peers round to see if the* NIGHT CLERK *is looking her way. His back is turned, so she silently takes a few steps that will get her to the main door without him seeing. The* NIGHT CLERK *looks up from his work, his back turned but a mirror in front of him. In the mirror we see his face looking up, the main door of the hotel, and* CLARA'*s rapidly disappearing figure.*)

EXT. PALAIS ROYAL. NIGHT

CLARA *now running back towards the bridge the opposite way, down the same arcade that we saw her in before, only now*

*running twice as fast. She runs frantically, covering the old
ground, her face set in panic and exhaustion.*

EXT. PONT DES ARTS. NIGHT
*The Pont des Arts is there, still in the night, its chain of lights
disappearing across the water. As* CLARA *reaches the north end of
it a group of students, smoking dope together at the end of the
bridge, steps in her way. She sidesteps, frightened one of them
will make a grab, but they let her go with some jeers. In the
middle of the bridge she stops. It is clear she cannot remember
where the murder took place. She is puzzled. She looks up and
down, bewildered. Lost. There is no sign of anything having
happened anywhere. The bag has gone.*

INT. ZINYAFSKIS' STAIRCASE. NIGHT
CLARA *stands outside the door to the Zinyafski building. She
presses the bell at ground level. A buzzer sounds and she
disappears up the staircase that leads to the Zinyafski apartment.
When she reaches the first floor, she comes to the apartment door
and finds it already open. She moves nervously towards it and
opens it, peering round.*

INT. ZINYAFSKIS' APARTMENT. NIGHT
CLARA *steps inside the apartment. There is a corridor stretching
away to one side and at the end of it she can see* MADAME
ZINYAFSKI *in her nightdress, having an argument, plainly about
the morality of* WALLACE *speaking to* CLARA *in the middle of
the night. Then she disappears into a bedroom.* CLARA *waits.
The light at the end of the corridor goes out and* WALLACE
*appears, coming down the corridor towards her. He is in pyjamas
and a woollen dressing-gown. He is very calm.*
WALLACE: I'm sorry. Are you all right?
CLARA: Yes. It's silly. I was panicking. I needed to talk.
(*He gestures to her to follow him through to another room
where they will not be overheard. She walks through with
him. There is a pause. He is looking at her quite
dispassionately, as if waiting to see the cause of her evident
distress, and yet determined she should reveal it herself.*)
I've lost my bag. It isn't . . . you haven't seen it? You

33

haven't got it?

(*There is an extraordinarily long pause. He is looking at her, yet it is impossible to tell what he is thinking. Whatever reason he thinks she has had for calling in the middle of the night has been disproved, yet he does not show it. Then quietly, after this alarming silence:*)

WALLACE: No. We can look.

(CLARA *starts talking quickly, nervously.*)

CLARA: I think . . . well, I . . . I had it when I left here.

WALLACE: You had it in the café. Remember, you offered to pay.

CLARA: That's right. That's right, yes, I did. I'd forgotten

that. Yes. And then I think . . . well, I did what I said I
was going to do. Do you remember? When I left you I
said I wanted to spend the night sitting under the Eiffel
Tower.

WALLACE: Did you?

CLARA: Oh, yes.

(*There's a slight pause.*)

Yes, I did.

(WALLACE *nods almost imperceptibly. He is very still, and
his tone is grave.*)

WALLACE: And did you have your bag?

CLARA: No. Well, yes. Perhaps I did. And no – not at the
end. That's when I realized. I'd been sitting for – what
time is it?

WALLACE: Four thirty.

CLARA: I suppose for a couple of hours – would that be
right? – just dreaming. There's a little garden where the
lights are that shine on the tower. It's such a lovely
garden and really I was feeling so relaxed, so free. Then
I just went for a stroll round the base of the tower,
looking up. Thought – oh, I've left the bag on the seat.

WALLACE: But it wasn't there?

CLARA: No.

(*There is a slight pause. He is still looking at her.*)

I'm sorry, I shouldn't have come really. I came because
I thought I might have left it here.

WALLACE: No.

(*Without saying any more, he walks past her into the
kitchen. He puts the light on. He takes out the coffee jug and
fills the kettle.* CLARA *watches him from the table, as he
moves confidently. His neat gestures as he works. She looks
apprehensive a moment, on the verge of saying something
more important.*)

CLARA: Also . . . to be honest . . . there was something
else . . .

WALLACE: Yes?

(*He turns, recognizing the seriousness of her tone. But just
behind her one of the children has appeared in the doorway of
the sitting room, and she calls out before* CLARA *can speak.*)

Ah, chérie, qu'est-ce que tu fais ici?

(*The* CHILD *is bleary-eyed, in her plain white nightdress.*)

GIRL: J'ai entendu des voix, oncle Wally.

WALLACE: Oh dear, goodness me . . .

(*But* VIOLET'S *voice is already coming from the corridor, as she turns the light on.*)

VIOLET: (*Voice over*) Stéphanie, where are you?

GIRL: On m'a éveillée, maman.

(VIOLET *appears, in plain pale pink pyjamas, pulling on a white cardigan as she comes. We notice how thin she is, how pale, and much more beautiful than we realized earlier.*)

VIOLET: Viens avec moi.

(*She expertly scoops the* CHILD *up in her arms and carries her past* CLARA *into the kitchen. As she passes,* VIOLET *smiles at* CLARA.)

You came back.

(*She puts the* CHILD *down on the kitchen counter. Then she gets a bottle of milk from the fridge and a brioche from a tin.*)

WALLACE: Elle a perdu sa pochette.

VIOLET: How terrible. (*She turns to* CLARA. *A simple statement of fact.*) Well, Wally will help.

(*She picks the* CHILD *up and puts her down on the sofa at the far end of the sitting room.* VIOLET *goes out. The* CHILD *sits on the sofa, lit by the lamp, eating her brioche and drinking her milk. The partition between the dining room and the sitting room has the effect of framing her from* CLARA'S *point of view, almost as if she were in a proscenium arch.* CLARA *watches her.*)

CLARA: Other people's lives always seem so attractive. Do we all feel that? Anyone's life but our own!

(WALLACE, *waiting for the kettle to boil, looks down at* CLARA *a moment. She is smiling.* VIOLET *has already returned.*)

VIOLET: Viens. Come on, piss off, go to bed.

(*The* CHILD *grins as if it has been a great lark to be up so early. She gets off the sofa and follows her mother out.* CLARA *smiles at* WALLACE.)

WALLACE: You were going to say . . . just before they came
   in . . . something else.
   (CLARA *looks at him, then away.*)
CLARA: Oh, yes. No, only . . . I have lost everything. Isn't it
   absurd? Bank book, traveller's cheques, credit cards. Is
   that coffee coming? Yes, the whole lot.

EXT. CAFÉ MAISON COLLIN. DAWN
CLARA *standing on the pavement watching as* WALLACE *talks to
the* BARMAN *in the café. It is not yet open for business, the
shutters are half raised and it is unlit. The tables are not yet out.
Then* WALLACE *comes out to join* CLARA.
WALLACE: He had a look. There are no bags.
CLARA: Oh, well. There we are.
WALLACE: Shall we report it?
CLARA: Report it? Oh, yes. (*She looks hesitantly at him.*) You
   mean to the police?
WALLACE: Well, surely, yes. I don't see how else you're
   going to get it back.

INT. POLICE STATION. DAY
CLARA *is sitting on a hard chair, much enjoying being the centre
of attention. Four or five gendarmes are buzzing around her,
discussing the possibility of getting her bag back. They are
enjoying it all too, because she looks interesting and attractive.*
WALLACE *turns from the argument, smiling.*
WALLACE: Are you getting this?
CLARA: Mostly.
WALLACE: They're saying, it's too early, can't expect
   anything. It's probably been stolen and you'll never see
   it again.
CLARA: Yes, well . . . j'ai pensé cela moi-même.
   (*She directs this deliberately at the oldest* GENDARME, *who
   smiles.*)
GENDARME: Vous avez promené la voie entière du Marais au
   Tour Eiffel?
CLARA: Oui.
GENDARME: C'est bien longue, ça.
WALLACE: He says . . .

37

CLARA: Yes, I know. It's a long way.

(*All her previous confidence and crispness has now returned. She turns and looks at the* GENDARME *and says very deliberately to him:*)

I didn't notice. Je n'ai pas remarqué.

GENDARME: Où avez-vous traversé la Seine?

CLARA: I did cross the river, I must have. I think by Notre-Dame. (*She is looking straight at the* GENDARME. *She pauses a moment.*) But then I never went near the river again.

(*Through the main door of the police station comes* SIR ARTHUR SANDERSON, *a very tall man with silver hair in his early fifties, and a younger man,* LAWRENCE, *equally thin, but more self-effacing. They are both in dark suits.*)

SANDERSON: Ah, Mrs Paige, how wonderful, we've found you. How distressing this thing must be. What an awful introduction to Paris. I promise you untypical. Lawrence . . .

(*He nods to the younger man who goes over and talks to the gendarmes.* CLARA *is looking at* WALLACE *ironically.*)

CLARA: Mr Sharp has been looking after me.

SANDERSON: (*Holding out his hand*) Foreign Office.

WALLACE: Good morning.

(*There is an embarrassed pause, the three of them stuck.*)

SANDERSON: Do you mind if I take Mrs Paige?

CLARA: You've been wonderful. Thank you.

(*She turns to go.* WALLACE *looks bewildered.*)

WALLACE: Are you off?

SANDERSON: Mrs Paige has to go now.

(*He is watching.* CLARA *has turned back and is looking at* WALLACE. *After a moment she speaks with great composure.*)

CLARA: Thank you. I trust I'll see you again.

(*And she turns and goes out.* WALLACE'*s face, frowning at the suddenness of her departure. He thinks.*)

EXT. PARIS STREET. DAY

SANDERSON *is standing on the pavement as* CLARA *comes out of the police station. The door of the car is held open by a chauffeur.*

SANDERSON *is handing her something from his wallet.*

SANDERSON: Here, this is a great thing. It's a government credit card. We have a wonderful deal. They just put your name on. We have what we call a special relationship. It used to be with America, now it's with American Express. (*He smiles and shows her the card.*) You can settle up when you get back to England.

CLARA: I've got rather nervous of losing things.
(*She pats the pocket of the dress which is now all she has to put things in.*)

SANDERSON: Shall I hold on to it for the moment? And we got you a float.

CLARA: I can manage that, I think.
(*She takes a roll of notes from him. She puts them in her pocket and gets into the car.*)

INT. EMBASSY CAR. DAY
SANDERSON *comes round the other side, getting into the car to join her.*

39

SANDERSON: I'm President of the Embassy's Amateur
     Dramatic Society. We've rather a hit on our hands. This
     is last night's take.
CLARA: How convenient.
SANDERSON: Well, we're doing *Sailor Beware*. The French
     just love it.
CLARA: I don't know it.
     (SANDERSON *signals the chauffeur to leave.*)
SANDERSON: (*Quietly*) I have the best part.
     (*The car slips off into the Paris traffic.*)

INT. MINISTÈRE DES AFFAIRES ÉTRANGÈRES. DAY
We track along beside SANDERSON *and* CLARA *to reveal the*
most extravagant and beautiful room, into which has been put an
enormous conference table covered in green baize. At its centre is
an artificial lily pond in sky-blue. All around, suited delegates are
waiting, conversing. Behind CLARA *and* SANDERSON *come*
LAWRENCE *and* SLATE-ESCOTT.
SANDERSON: There's very little chance of this conference
     coming to anything. There've been thirty of these
     things. They never work. French government is in
     permanent thrall to French farmers. They produce too
     much food and that's the end of it. And no one here
     dares tell them to stop.
     (*They take their seats at the table.*)

INT. MINISTÈRE DES AFFAIRES ÉTRANGÈRES. DAY
Six or seven British delegates stand up as CLARA *slips into her*
place at the table. At once LAWRENCE *appears beside her with a*
big pile of files, a foot high.
LAWRENCE: These are the documents I think you'll find
     useful. The tariff agreements.
CLARA: Ah, good.
LAWRENCE: The Brussels wine deal. The Green Pound
     transfer balance ratification agreement.
     (*He thumbs through the files. She's nodding.*)
     Self-explanatory. (*Smiles.*) The Minister relies on you.
     (CLARA *smiles too at this tacit admission of the Minister's*
     abilities. She reaches for the headphones and puts them on.)

CLARA: So. When do we start?
(*At once there is a blare of trumpets and a row of heralds in historic costume stand at the door. Everyone in the room stands up. Suddenly a cigar stub lands with a hiss in the artificial lily pond at the centre of the table.* CLARA *looks up alarmed. She sees* ADAM GILLVRAY. *He is looking at her steadily and, now she sees him, he winks.*)
VOICE: Mesdames, messieurs, le Président de la République.

EXT. MINISTÈRE DES AFFAIRES ÉTRANGÈRES. DAY
Down a formal flight of stairs come thirty or forty suited men who

41

file with absolute neatness into position as for a school photo. In the distance a tractor is unloading apples in great quantities in the middle of the road. An anti-EEC demonstration of French farmers. The politicians resolutely take no notice, talking among themselves. SANDERSON *nudges* CLARA.

SANDERSON: Look at that. Bloody barbarians.

> *(They are now being rounded up by CRS police in full riot gear with machine-guns.* CLARA *smiles. A full-scale riot begins in the distance. Then the CRS who are standing in front of the podium part and allow in a photographer.* CLARA *is the only woman among them as the photograph is taken.)*

EXT. HOTEL. EVENING

The chauffeur-driven car arrives outside the Hôtel and CLARA, *who is now alone in the car, gets out. She smiles and waves at the chauffeur. She has a selection of files and documents tucked under her arm, and is still wearing the same dress. She goes into the hotel.*

INT. HOTEL LOBBY. EVENING

We follow behind CLARA *as she walks towards the desk. It is as if she is becoming tense at the idea of approaching the spot where last night she behaved so peculiarly. But as the clerk turns at the reception we see that it is a different person from last night. It is a* YOUNGER CLERK.

CLARA: J'ai perdu ma clef. Deux cent quarante.

YOUNG CLERK: Attendez.

> *(He runs his finger along the line of keys. When he gets to 240, there is a thick wad of notes stuffed there. He takes them at once.)*

Ah, madame, on vous appelle toute la journée. You have many messages. They are very urgent.

> *(She takes the telephone notes from him and looks. She looks frightened. She hands one quickly back to him.)*

CLARA: Please can you get me this number in London.

YOUNG CLERK: Yes. You must wait in the booth.

> *(He nods at the corridor where she hid last night. She goes as he turns to the switchboard to dial. She goes and stands*

outside the booth, a look of anxiety on her face. Then the
phone rings. She puts the files down in the booth and
snatches the receiver.)
PAULINE: (*Voice over*) Oh, Clara, thank goodness we've
found you.
CLARA: What's happened?
PAULINE: (*Voice over*) It's Simon.
(*There is a pause.*)
CLARA: What?
PAULINE: (*Voice over*) He's been taken to hospital.
CLARA: What was it?
PAULINE: (*Voice over*) Appendicitis.
CLARA: And is he all right?

INT. PAULINE'S HOUSE. EVENING
PAULINE'*s face in close-up, evening light cutting across her face.*
You have no impression of where she is, simply of a new note of
concern.
PAULINE: Clara, you should know . . . we've been trying to
get you. Ever since the middle of last night. I gather . . .
well, they said you never came back.

INT. HOTEL. EVENING
CLARA: (*Lost for a reply*) I must . . . I just . . . I must be
with him. All I need . . . look . . . (*She looks down at the*
money SANDERSON *gave her. It is screwed up in her hand,*
wet with sweat.) It's just a silly thing, I'm short of
money. I'll need to go to the Embassy. Then I'll get the
first plane. Tell him when he wakes . . . three hours. I
can do it in three hours.
PAULINE: (*Voice over*) Eight o'clock?
CLARA: With luck. And Pauline . . . (*She pauses a moment.*)
Tell the boy I love him very much.

INT. EMBASSY. EVENING
CLARA *waiting in the main hallway of the British Embassy. It is*
a formidable, marbled building which has been converted to serve
its public purposes. Various people are sitting round waiting on
the various remains of business at the end of the day. CLARA *is*

pacing up and down when LAWRENCE *arrives from inside the Embassy.*

CLARA: Oh, Lawrence, thank you. I'll tell you, there's something. A credit card. Sir Arthur offered it to me today. And I meant to take it.

LAWRENCE: Of course. We could have sent it over. (*He looks at her a moment, as if slightly puzzled by the way she is still in the same dress with her roll of cash in her hand.*) Why don't you come through?

INT. EMBASSY CORRIDOR. EVENING

LAWRENCE *walking* CLARA *along the corridor which leads from the reception area of the Embassy. It is quite dark but very elaborately decorated.* LAWRENCE *is talking politely but* CLARA *is not really listening.*

LAWRENCE: Everyone says, 'Oh, you are in Paris, how jammy. All that wonderful food.' But some days I'd actually kill for an English pork sausage. In fact, a friend of mine kindly sends me some out.
(*They head up some stairs,* LAWRENCE *still talking.*)
And landscape. The French do have landscape. And a lot of it, if you're honest, is really very nice. If you like canals. But they don't have countryside. Countryside is something you only really get in England. Countryside to me means oaks.
(*They are passing offices on either side of the corridor. At an open door to the left, a* GIRL *is sitting. She is about eighteen, slim, dark, in white dungarees and yellow sneakers. As* CLARA *passes, she looks up.* LAWRENCE *is still talking as he turns into the office he is headed for.* CLARA *is about to follow him in, when she pauses at the door, as if remembering something she has seen but not registered. She stops and turns. At the opposite office door the* GIRL *has got up from the chair and come to the door jamb where she is looking across at* CLARA, *plainly recognizing her. They are about seven feet apart. Before the* GIRL *can speak,* CLARA *slips into the office she is heading for.*)

44

INT. EMBASSY OFFICE. EVENING
This is the outer office which leads to Sanderson's larger one.
Normally there is a secretary but she has gone home. The walls
are lined with books, and the effect is more like a small private
drawing room than an office. LAWRENCE *has already gone*
across to the inner door and is knocking on it. SANDERSON *is*
heard to say 'Come in'.

LAWRENCE: Hold on.
  (*He goes through.* CLARA *is left alone. She thinks a*
  moment, then goes to sneak a look back through the door.
  The GIRL *has returned to her seat in the opposite office, and*
  is now sitting patiently, her face in profile to us. CLARA
  stares at her, quite still. Silently, LAWRENCE *has*
  returned.)
  Here you are.
  (CLARA *stares at him now. He is holding out an American*
  Express card.)

CLARA: Oh, thank you. (*There is a pause.*) Do you know that
  girl over there?

LAWRENCE: Yes, I do. Actually I've been asked to help look
  after it. She's a girl whose father's disappeared.
  (CLARA *takes the card and moves a couple of paces away*
  from him, turned away.)

CLARA: I see.

LAWRENCE: She came in completely hysterical. On no
  evidence. I mean he's only been gone less than twenty-
  four hours. Could be anywhere. But I think we've
  managed to calm her down a bit –

CLARA: You mean – what – she was with him?

LAWRENCE: Yes.

CLARA: In Paris?

LAWRENCE: Why?

CLARA: No, I mean . . . (*She looks at him, then away. She*
  walks to the other side of the room.) Most people who want
  . . . who have some reason to vanish . . . well, they
  don't do it with their daughter around.

LAWRENCE: We don't know he's vanished. It could be an
  accident. (*He frowns a moment, looking at her.*) Are you
  all right?

(She smiles as if to say she's fine.)
CLARA: May I use your phone?

INT. HOSPITAL. EVENING
*The children's ward of a large, modern London hospital. It is
wonderfully comforting and serene. Also at the moment it is very
quiet.* SIMON *is dozing in his bed, a light above him, as above
all other beds. But we only see him in long shot, for a* NURSE
has fetched GERALD *and is leading him to the desk to take a
phone call. He is in a suit.*
CLARA: *(Voice over)* Gerald.
   (He does not answer.)
   Gerald. It's Clara.
   (There is a pause.)
GERALD: Yes?
CLARA: *(Voice over)* Pauline said the operation's over.
GERALD: Yes.
CLARA: *(Voice over)* And?
GERALD: He's doing fine.
CLARA: *(Voice over)* Is he awake?
GERALD: Just. He asked for you.

INT. EMBASSY. EVENING
CLARA *is standing alone in the office with the phone in her
hands.*
CLARA: Look, I . . .
   *(She looks to the door, which she has deliberately left ajar.
   Across the corridor she can see the open door of the opposite
   office where Swanton's daughter,* JENNY, *is sitting
   patiently. Unobserved,* CLARA *keeps an eye on her.)*
   When I spoke to Pauline I said I'd be coming right over.
   I said I'd get a plane. And this is what I was intending.
   But you have to trust me. Just for the moment I have to
   stay in Paris.
   (There is silence at the other end. CLARA *looks again to the
   open door. The* GIRL *has not moved.)*
   Gerald. Gerald.
   (There is a pause.)
GERALD: *(Voice over, low)* Who is this man?

CLARA: What man?

GERALD (*Voice over*) The man you were out with. We called
 you, we called you all night.

CLARA: Gerald, it's *me*. Does it seem likely?

(*There is a silence. The* GIRL *is brought a cup of tea by a
 man in a suit. She smiles and takes it. Now* GERALD
 reluctantly and rather bitterly concedes.)

GERALD: (*Voice over*) Who is the man who rings the flat?

CLARA: What?

GERALD: (*Voice over*) A couple of times. A man has rung
 here and put the phone down.

CLARA: Gerald, I know . . . I know what you're talking
 about. But I have seen to it. (*She is choosing her words
 with great care.*) I promise you that will never happen
 again.

INT. HOSPITAL. EVENING

A nurse goes by, carrying flowers. GERALD *smiles at her
absently, turns away, because what he is about to say is so
intimate and sincere.*

GERALD: Clara, I've been a bloody fool. You know that. (*He
 looks down the ward to the distant, sleeping figure of the*
 BOY.) When you see this little boy, you realize. I love
 him. I love you. We've both been beastly and careless of
 each other. Me as well as you. You forget why you first
 married. And the whole purpose of your life. When
 something like this happens you realize we must make
 an effort. Please come back to me. I want to see you
 tonight.

INT. EMBASSY. EVENING

CLARA *has tears in her eyes now, from* GERALD's *tone on the
telephone.*

CLARA: Look I . . . you know I want to . . . For some time
 I've wanted to . . . settle things down. It's just . . .
 (*She looks across. The* GIRL *is putting her tea down on the
 seat next to her and is picking up her things as if to go.*)
 I can't leave Paris right now.

47

(There is a pause. When GERALD *speaks it is with a terrible quiet viciousness.)*

GERALD: *(Voice over)* Work. That's all there is for you. Eyes straight ahead. Getting on. The idea of an affair even, how ridiculous. Not you. Not Clara. Not the new model citizen. Unthinkable. And even now when your son is lying there . . .

(The GIRL *has now got up and is about to leave.* CLARA *interrupts* GERALD.)*

CLARA: Please, I'm sorry, I'm afraid I have to go.

GERALD: *(Voice over)* What can be more important than your own son's illness? Come back tonight or I will never forgive you.

(But she has already put down the phone. She goes quickly to the door. The GIRL *is now some way down the corridor. She is lame and walks with a noticeable limp.* CLARA *calls out:)*

CLARA: Jenny!

(She turns round.)

JENNY: Hello.

CLARA: I apologize. Just now. I didn't recognize you.

JENNY: That's all right.

CLARA: I haven't seen you since you were at school.

(She smiles. They are a long way apart. So CLARA *has to walk all the way down the corridor to her.* JENNY *stands waiting.* CLARA *gets nearer. Now she is only a few feet away.)*

What are you doing here?

INT. LEFT BANK HOTEL: CORRIDOR. EVENING
CLARA *and* JENNY *coming together up the stairs of a tiny Left Bank hotel and along a little garret corridor. It is very poky. Some red carpet is threadbare on the floor. They come to the grey door of one of the rooms.*

INT. LEFT BANK HOTEL: SWANTON'S ROOM. EVENING
JENNY *unlocks the door. Inside there are the signs of Michael Swanton's occupancy. It is the tiniest room, with a single bed, and an attic window.* JENNY *turns on the light.* CLARA *comes in, and stands a moment in the room, then starts to look at*

48

*Swanton's belongings. There is an Antler suitcase open on the
small luggage table. There are a couple of nylon shirts, some
socks, a pulp novel.* CLARA *lifts the shirts but there is nothing
underneath. She looks to the dressing table, on which there are a
pair of old, but silver, hairbrushes and some cologne. She opens a
cupboard. There is a single dark brown suit hanging there. She
looks a moment, then closes the door.* JENNY *has sat down on the
edge of the bed, and is watching* CLARA *move through the things
in the room.*

JENNY: I know what you're thinking. It's not much of a life.

CLARA: I didn't say that.

JENNY: I wouldn't blame you. We're broke.

CLARA: Yes.

JENNY: That's why I'm frightened. I think he's done himself
in.

(CLARA *looks at her a moment, thoughtfully.*)

CLARA: I used to love coming round to look after you. I
remember being so jealous of your parents. Because at
the time I had no children of my own. And you had that
lovely house in Walsall. When they needed a babysitter
I'd volunteer.

JENNY: I liked your strictness.

CLARA: Was I strict? I wonder.

JENNY: I was allowed no excuses. Even though I was lame. I
was so bored with everyone's expressions of concern.

(CLARA *smiles.* JENNY *is reaching into her pocket for her
wallet.*)

I still have a picture.

CLARA: Oh, really?

JENNY: Yes. Look.

(*A tattered photograph of a group in an English garden. It's
the mid-seventies. Michael and Janet Swanton are standing,
with the five-year-old Jenny on Janet's arm. Gerald, much
younger, has his arm round Clara, who has turned to laugh
at something he is saying.*)

Look at you and Gerald.

CLARA: Mmm.

JENNY: So loving.

CLARA: Yes. He was once a very passionate man. (*She thinks*

49

a moment, then moves away.) Does your father ever mention me?

JENNY: Dad? Only in passing.

CLARA: Uh-huh.

JENNY: Once or twice lately.

CLARA: But I haven't seen him at all.

(CLARA *looks across to see if* JENNY *will confirm or deny this.* JENNY *has sat down on the bed, against the pillows and is now getting out a cigarette, offering one to* CLARA, *who shakes her head.*)

It must be four years since I last saw Michael. It got a bit difficult. At the . . . well, when the business went down, then things between us got very hard. (*She waits a moment.*) I wanted . . . I wondered whether he's said anything to you.

(JENNY *frowns, on a tack of her own.*)

JENNY: Weren't you technically still directors?

CLARA: There'd been some confusion. Our names were meant to have been removed at Companies House. But it turned out they hadn't. Michael kindly said nothing.

(JENNY *just smokes, not reacting.* CLARA *is quiet.*)

But of course our position was ethically correct.

(*She moves to the little garret window of the room.*)

JENNY: Also he told me Gerald gave him wrong information.

CLARA: Really? (*She turns, as if thinking about this for the first time.*) I'd never heard that.

JENNY: When he took over the firm. What's it called? Creative accountancy. Dad didn't get a true picture of what debts he was inheriting.

CLARA: If that's so, when he found out, why didn't he go back and say something to Gerald?

(JENNY *takes another puff at her cigarette.*)

JENNY: Because he's too nice.

(CLARA *looks at her, the room darkening now.*)

People's luck marks them. I've heard so many people being rude about Dad. Really his crime is he's in need and it shows. So he sweats a lot and asks people for favours. So people say he's shifty. They say he's embarrassing. But what's embarrassing is he's got no money.

CLARA: It's unfair.

JENNY: Oh yes. But it means he'll never get back. (JENNY *has tears in her eyes now. As if to fight them, she stubs out her cigarette and gets off the bed.*) Will you stay? Just for this evening?

(CLARA *nods.*)

I'd like to be able to talk.

INT. LEFT BANK HOTEL: SWANTON'S ROOM. EVENING

CLARA *sits alone in the darkening room, the light bulb making almost no impact above her. Then she gets up and closes Swanton's suitcase. She straightens it on the rack. Then she puts his two silver hairbrushes neatly together on the dressing table. She turns the light off.*

INT. LEFT BANK HOTEL: CORRIDOR/JENNY'S ROOM.
EVENING
JENNY *is changing in the next room. She has put on a smarter
pair of trousers and has a white vest on top.* CLARA's *hand
pushes the door open, and* JENNY, *not realizing* CLARA *is there,
has stopped and is sobbing, her back to us. The room is even
plainer than Swanton's. She looks painfully thin.* CLARA *moves
into the room and takes hold of her. They embrace, both deeply
moved.*

INT. PARIS RESTAURANT. NIGHT
CLARA *in the little corridor of a restaurant that leads to the
telephone. She has got out her British Airways timetable, and is
thumbing through it. We see the page for the* PARIS–LONDON
*flights. The last one is at ten o'clock. She looks at a clock. It says
nine fifteen. She sighs resignedly, then looks into the restaurant.
There* JENNY *is sitting alone at a table laid for two.* CLARA

*walks across to her. The restaurant is cheerful but smart. Waiters
are in long white aprons and have bow ties. There are many
mirrors. The place is very full and exuberant and although it
affects to be bohemian, there is a smell of money in the air. They
both have lobster, beautiful, colourful, dead. There are two kinds
of wine and sparkling water in good glasses.* JENNY *is not
eating.*

CLARA: Eat.

JENNY: I can't. I'm so unhappy.

> (CLARA *looks round the restaurant, as if nervous of being
> seen not to eat the food here.*)

What's that heresy they taught us at school?

CLARA: I don't know.

JENNY: Somewhere in the world for every bit of happiness,
somewhere else there's a bit of unhappiness.

> (CLARA *takes a nervous look for a waiter.*)

It's called Manichaean. For every rise there's a fall.

> (CLARA *looks at her seriously, deciding to take her on.*)

CLARA: Look . . .

JENNY: You think I blame you. You think Dad blames you.
But he doesn't. If he took a dud firm, it's nobody's fault
but his own. Even if he was given the wrong figures, not
told the whole picture – a warehouse full of goods was
entered twice; sold and not sold apparently – even if
that's true, let's say it is, if he accepted it, then as far as
I'm concerned that's his liability.

> (*She looks fiercely at* CLARA, *proud, unbending.* CLARA
> *looks nervous of her intensity.*)

And if he were here, he would tell you that's how he
feels as well.

> (CLARA *smiles as if to agree, in the hope of calming* JENNY
> *down a little.*)

He even has – this is the extraordinary thing – he has
the piece of paper Gerald gave him with the figures
on . . .

CLARA: Where is it?

JENNY: This is my father. He put it away in a drawer. All he
said was, 'My foolishness'. (*Tears have appeared in her
eyes. She is now quietly hysterical.*) Yes. I love him very

much.

(CLARA *looks again for a waiter, as* JENNY *pushes her plate back.*)

And now what? We come over here. For *me*. He came for me. He wanted me to learn Italian, because I long to work in fashion. He said, learn the business, spend the summer with a family in Milan. With what? With what, Daddy? He said, I'll sell the car. So I asked him to come with me, just to give my mother a break. And I got the wrong bloody platform.

CLARA: What?

JENNY: We're not even meant to be in Paris.

CLARA: But that's not possible.

(CLARA *sits appalled as* JENNY *begins to shout.*)

JENNY: We got the wrong train at Boulogne. I led him to the wrong fucking platform. (*She gestures violently with her hand. A wine glass goes over, smashing on the tiled floor. Now she bursts, at full pitch.*) I'm meant to be in fucking Milan. Not in this fucking nightmare. Where is he? Where has he gone?

(CLARA *gets up in alarm. A* WAITER *has already come over.*)

WAITER: Est-ce que je peux vous aider?

CLARA: No, really, honestly, it's not to do with anything . . .

(JENNY *has stood up and is now shouting at* CLARA.)

JENNY: You tell me! Somebody tell me! What do you want? What does everyone want? We sit here and eat dinner as if nothing's happened?

(CLARA *is furious with her for making a scene.*)

CLARA: Jenny. I came out to *help* you . . .

JENNY: Jesus Christ, I'm going to go mad.

(*She limps furiously off, crashing into another table as she goes. The diners' glasses tumble. The whole restaurant is now watching this scene.* CLARA, *swallowing her anger, first addresses* JENNY's *back, then the* WAITER.)

CLARA: I'm sorry, no, look, wait. (*To the* WAITER) Hold on, attendez, je reviens . . .

(*But* JENNY *is already out the door.* CLARA *turns back to the* WAITER, *wanting to follow but having to pay first.*)

Actually I'll pay. Do you . . . (*She has taken out the American Express card.*) Oh, God, it'll take so long. How much is it?

WAITER: Attendez. I find out.

(CLARA *drops some damp notes on the table. But the* WAITER *has already gone to get the correct bill. A couple in their early sixties have come over from their table. The* MAN *has a plaid jacket on.*)

MAN: Can we help you? We're American.

CLARA: No, thank you. It was someone . . . I didn't know very well.

MAN: She really looks crazy.

(CLARA *turns away, darting a smile at him. Waiters are on all fours clearing up the mess. The* AMERICAN *stands waiting.*)

CLARA: Yes. Well, that's what happens when you try and help someone else.

EXT. BOULEVARD ST GERMAIN. NIGHT

From outside we see CLARA *coming out of the restaurant, once more composed. The picture of swift efficiency as she swerves through the tables to make her way out. She comes out on to the pavement. She looks up and down the boulevard for signs of* JENNY. *The evening crowds are out, on their way to cinemas and restaurants. Gangs of youths walk by. She stands looking. But* JENNY *has gone.*

INT. HOTEL: BEDROOM. NIGHT

CLARA *comes into her hotel room. The lights are already on. There is a presentation of fruit by the bed. It is warm, luxurious, creamy and comforting. She takes off her shoes and lies a moment on the bed, exhausted. Then undoes the two top buttons of her dress and goes into the bathroom. The sound of the shower being turned on. A moment later she reappears, walking across to the case at the other side of the room to get out some shampoo. As she walks, she suddenly slows down. By the time she reaches the case she is listening. It is as if she knows what is going to happen before it does. She reaches down into the case, gets out the shampoo, turns. She stands listening. Nothing.*

55

INT. HOTEL: BEDROOM. NIGHT

She comes out of the bathroom in a white dressing-gown. She returns some lotions to the table. She goes to the bed. She takes off her dressing-gown. Underneath she has silk pyjamas on. She gets into bed. Open on the bed is a briefcase full of official papers. She puts on a pair of glasses, glances at one, puts it aside. She turns and looks at the phone. Silence. She reaches and puts out the light.

INT. HOTEL: BEDROOM. NIGHT

Darkness. CLARA *asleep. The phone rings. She jumps awake, scrambling desperately for the phone. But then, when she has picked it up, she pauses. Holds it out. Says nothing. A pause.*
VOICE: Hello. How are you?
    (*No reaction from* CLARA.)
    (*Very deliberately*) I know who you are.
    (CLARA *holds the receiver away from her ear, then puts it down quietly. She sits in the bed alone.*)

INT. ZINYAFSKIS' APARTMENT. NIGHT

WALLACE *is answering the phone in his bedroom. You cannot really see where you are. The dim light reveals him to be in a white T-shirt and pants, like an American.*
CLARA: (*Voice over*) Wally, it's Clara.
WALLACE: Clara.
CLARA: (*Voice over*) I'm at the hotel.
WALLACE: I see. What d'you mean? It's the middle of the night. Why will you only speak to me in the middle of the night?
    (*He is smiling, attentive for sounds in the household.*)
CLARA: (*Voice over*) Wally, I want to see you.
WALLACE: All right.

INT. HOTEL: BEDROOM. NIGHT

CLARA *sits alone on the side of the bed. Tears are pouring down her face. She begins to cry, moaning softly, sobbing.*

INT. HOTEL: BEDROOM. NIGHT

CLARA *opens the door of her room a little. All trace of the tears has gone, her face wiped clean.* WALLACE *stands outside.*

CLARA: There you are.

WALLACE: I had to bribe the night porter.

(*She closes the door and goes to sit on the edge of the bed in her silk pyjamas.*)

CLARA: I was frightened you'd have gone.

WALLACE: Did you find your handbag?

CLARA: No. It seems to be lost.

(*She gets up and kisses him. They look at each other. Then she kisses him again. He puts his hand inside her pyjamas on her breast. They both smile. He steps back and goes to take his jacket off. She goes and lies on the bed. He smiles.*)

WALLACE: What happened?

CLARA: Oh, you know . . . just thinking it over.

(*He turns in trousers and shirt. He moves towards her. He smiles as they lie back. We travel up the whole length of their bodies. As we reach their faces, CLARA reaches out with her hand and takes the phone off the hook. We go right into the phone. There is dark.*)

INT. HOTEL: BATHROOM. NIGHT

Later. The darkness held. Then a crack of light from the window reveals that we are in the bathroom. WALLACE *is carrying his clothes. He puts them on the floor. He is very quiet. He is naked.* CLARA's *voice from the door, where she stands, also naked.*

CLARA: Where are you going?

WALLACE: I have to go.

CLARA: Why?

WALLACE: My business. I have business in Rennes.

(*She moves towards him. She reaches out and touches the side of his face. Accidently the blind is unsettled and it shoots up with an enormous noise. They both jump a little, then smile.*)

CLARA: Were you sloping off?

WALLACE: Not really. Well, yes. Being tactful.

(*They both smile, at the absurdity of it.*)

CLARA: I really want you.

WALLACE: Good. Then I'll stay.

(*She moves towards him. They embrace. She presses him against the wall, with a deep kiss.*)

INT. HOTEL: BEDROOM. NIGHT

CLARA's *face, a little wild, damp against the pillow.* WALLACE *close.*

CLARA: What's that you do?

WALLACE: What? That? (*He smiles.*) Don't you like it?
    (*She arches back against the bed.*)

CLARA: I don't know.

INT. HOTEL: BEDROOM. NIGHT

Later. CLARA *is sitting up on the bed, up against the headboard.* WALLACE *is in an opposite armchair. They are both still naked. There is almost no light. The atmosphere is very easy between them.*

CLARA: I married early.

WALLACE: I see.

CLARA: I was really quite young. I was influenced by people I
    knew. Contemporaries. Friends who seemed to make a
    mess of their lives. I don't like mess. Promiscuity. (*She
    frowns.*) I wanted to avoid all the awful sloppiness people
    get into. Friends from school became hippies. No shape
    to their lives.
    (WALLACE *is watching her, fascinated.*)
    A lot of us now are tired with all the old excuses. Just
    get on with things. There's been far too much living off
    the state. People get soft. They always think there's
    someone who'll solve their problems for them. I hate
    that softness.
    (WALLACE *is watching her steadily.*)

WALLACE: I see.

CLARA: People should make their own decisions. If you do
    something, you must live with the consequences.

WALLACE: Goodness. Is that what you do?
    (*She is looking down. She looks up at him a moment, as if
    he saw right through her.*)

CLARA: Don't you agree?

WALLACE: It sounds very harsh. You're not like that.

CLARA: Aren't I?

WALLACE: No, I don't think so. Or if you are, you have

another side.

CLARA: Do I?

WALLACE: Yes, I think so. I've seen it. You've shown it to me.

CLARA: Have I?

(*They look at each other, full of tenderness.*)

Why are you smiling?

WALLACE: You're my first naked Tory.

(*She smiles.*)

CLARA: And you? Do you have two sides to you?

WALLACE: I change according to who I'm with.

CLARA: And with me?

(*He smiles.*)

WALLACE: No. I'm not telling you yet.

INT. HOTEL: BEDROOM. NIGHT

Now she is curled up in the bed, on his chest. He can't see her face.

WALLACE: You're crying.

CLARA: No. No, I'm not crying.

(*He runs his finger beneath her eye.*)

WALLACE: What's this?

CLARA: Sweat.

WALLACE: Ah. Do you sweat from your eyes?

(*She turns and looks at him.*)

Don't look like that.

CLARA: Why not?

WALLACE: Because then I can't leave you.

CLARA: (*Smiling*) Oh, right. Then I'll do it again. (*She looks at him.*) Is that what you fear?

WALLACE: Mmm?

CLARA: Not being free? Not being able to go off on your own?

WALLACE: I always have.

(CLARA *turns away, smiling.*)

Now *you're* laughing.

CLARA: I'm happy, that's all.

59

INT. HOTEL: BEDROOM. NIGHT

CLARA *gets out of the bed.* WALLACE *is asleep. She pulls on a dressing-gown. She goes across to his jacket and takes out the napkin with the drawing of her on it. She looks at it. She takes it across to the desk, and reaches for a pen.*

INT. PARIS CAFÉ. DAY

A bright Paris morning. A huge café with WALLACE *and* CLARA *seen across rows of empty tables, lingering over coffee and croissants.* CLARA *puts down the American Express card.*

CLARA: It's on the government. Look, it has a special code.
    (*She beams happily. The card reads* H.M. GOVERNMENT, *then underneath* CLARA H. PAIGE.)

WALLACE: So, are you heading back to your conference?

CLARA: No. I can't. I've got to go back to England. My . . .
    (*She stops dead.*)

WALACE: What?

CLARA: No, my son has been ill.

WALLACE: What d'you mean?

CLARA: He had appendicitis.

WALLACE: When?

CLARA: Oh, you know. Recently. (*She pauses, knowing how bad this sounds. Then, reluctantly*) The night before last.

WALLACE: You're joking. Why haven't you been with him?

CLARA: It's tricky. I only heard last night.

WALLACE: But why aren't you going?

CLARA: (*Beginning to get angry*) I am going. I'm just about to go. I'm just about to call. All right? (*She looks at him angrily, all her bad conscience coming out as aggression.*) He was ill. He had an operation. And now he's all right.
    (*The waiter comes and takes the bill and the card. They sit across the table from one another, angry and miserable. A desultory game of pinball begins behind them. Then* WALLACE *shakes his head.*)

WALLACE: I don't understand.

CLARA: You just have to trust me. There's a whole lot of things . . . there are things I can't explain. Last night I just thought . . . oh, God, I mean of course I wanted to

go home. Are you mad? Of course I did. But the operation was over. Simon was fine. (*She is suddenly very quiet. She looks him straight in the eye.*) And I wanted to spend just one night with you.
(*He looks straight back at her, searchingly.*)
Was that wrong? You must tell me. Tell me please.
Look at me, Wally. Was that the wrong thing to do?

INT. HOTEL: BEDROOM. DAY
They are making love again, but this time much more violently. We are across the room from them. Small howls of pain from CLARA, *as if* WALLACE *were trying to get the truth out of her.*

EXT. RIVER BANK. DAY
Swanton's body face down in the water, travelling downriver. Then we see an idyllic country scene, outside Paris. The river bank; a CHILD *playing, picking up a stick to throw in the water; her parents walking along the path nearby. The* CHILD *sees the shape in the water.*
CHILD: Eh, maman, regarde-la.
(*The* MOTHER *stops, sees nothing.*)
MOTHER: Viens, chérie, c'est rien.
(*The* CHILD *runs and catches up with its parents. Swanton's body is caught in a sudden strong stream and carried fast away and into the distance.*)

INT. HOTEL: BEDROOM. DAY
Close in now, as CLARA, *sweating, suddenly cries out.*

INT. HOSPITAL. DAY
SIMON *sitting in bed, watching television. Then he looks down the ward.* CLARA *is standing by the other end. He calls all the way down.*
SIMON: Mum! Mum!
(CLARA *runs the full length of the ward towards him. They hug. She begins to cry.*)

CLARA: Oh, my God, Simon, I've missed you.
(*A passing* NURSE *smiles at* SIMON. CLARA *is unloading presents.*)
NURSE: Your mother's back, Simon.
CLARA: Are you all right? I brought you these. And this, look.
(*There are chocolates from Fauchons, and a small gold Eiffel Tower on a lurid orange base.* SIMON *beams and takes it.*)
SIMON: Imran Khan made a hundred.
CLARA: Did he?
SIMON: It was brilliant.
(CLARA *has tears in her eyes.*)
CLARA: Yes. (*She turns and sees* PAULINE *standing at the end of the bed.*) My dear, there you are.
PAULINE: How are you?
CLARA: Why, I'm fine.
(PAULINE *just looks at her.* CLARA *picks up the meaning of the look and turns.* GERALD *is at the bottom of the ward. She walks towards him. At the last moment she reaches out her hand towards him.*)
Hello, darling, I'm back. He's been so brave. I just can't wait to take him home.

INT. FLAT: SIMON'S BEDROOM. NIGHT
SIMON *is lying in his bunk bed. His room is neat, like the rest of the flat. A single lamp beside the bed. Immediately behind him, a Rousseau-like painting of a leopard in a forest. He is very quiet.*
SIMON: Will you tell me a story?
CLARA: Yes, of course I will. Any story?
SIMON: As long as someone dies.
CLARA: (*Smiles*) Why that?
SIMON: So I can do it. Look.
(*He pretends to lie dead, his eyes closed.*)
CLARA: That's terrible. Your eyes are fluttering.
SIMON: I'm thinking dead.
(*She kisses him. He stays dead.*)
CLARA: It's not the same thing.

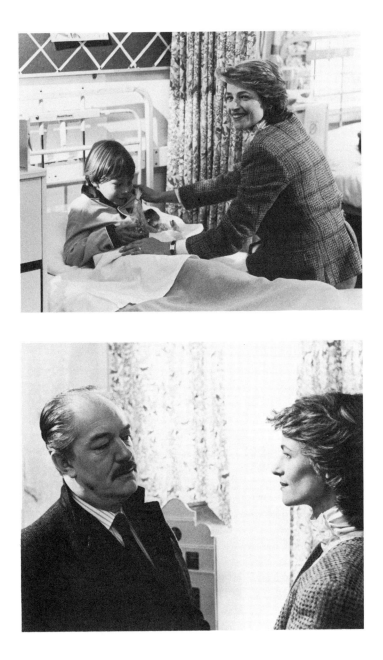

(*She puts the little model of the Eiffel Tower on the pillow beside him.*)

INT. FLAT: CORRIDOR. NIGHT
SIMON *asleep now, seen from the doorway, his light still burning beside him.* CLARA, *standing against the door jamb, looks down the corridor towards her own bedroom, from which light falls into the darkened corridor. A moment to prepare, and then she moves.*

INT. FLAT: BEDROOM. NIGHT
GERALD *is sitting in bed, reading a novel. He has half-moon glasses on and has a cardigan over his pyjamas.* CLARA *comes in, trying to seem casual, then sits down on the piano stool at the end of the bed. He does not look up.*
GERALD: Well?
CLARA: I think we should divorce.
GERALD: Oh yes? (*He does not look up from his book.*) Why?
CLARA: It's obvious, isn't it? None of us can live in this atmosphere.
GERALD: Really? We always have.
(*He is apparently mild. But as soon as* CLARA *speaks, he interrupts.*)

CLARA: Look . . .

GERALD: Oh, yes, I can see it would suit you. I'm an
embarrassment. I'm getting old. I've seen you do it to
everyone, since you were a girl. If they don't shape up,
kick 'em out.

CLARA: That's not fair.

GERALD: (*Suddenly quiet*) I'll fight you for Simon. Oh, yes. In
public. In the courts. In the papers. I've got nothing to
lose. But you have. I'll get him.

CLARA: You wouldn't.

GERALD: I'll say what sort of mother you were. You didn't
come home when he was in hospital. (*He looks at her.*)
Well, did you? It doesn't look good.

CLARA: (*Suddenly violent*) What do you *want*?

GERALD: Very little. (*He goes back to his book, with a little
smile.*) If you've got a man, I would like to know.

INT. GILLVRAY'S OFFICES. DAY

*A fine Georgian House in Bloomsbury. It has been converted into
offices on an open plan on the ground floor. A great deal of high-
tech machinery in old-fashioned surroundings. Computers, word
processors, stainless steel and glass desks. Six girls at work, all
young and busy.* ADAM GILLVRAY *is standing at the back, in
Jermyn Street shirtsleeves and braces, looking over a girl's
shoulder at a word processor. He greets* CLARA *as she arrives.*

CLARA: Adam, there you are.

GILLVRAY: How good of you to come.

CLARA: I was delighted.

  (*They go upstairs together, round a big circular staircase at
  the centre of the house.*)

GILLVRAY: I hear you did well in Paris.

CLARA: I did nothing.

GILLVRAY: There are times when nothing is best.

INT. FIRST FLOOR OFFICE. DAY

GILLVRAY *is standing in an empty room, his back against the
fireplace. The surroundings are startlingly modern.*

GILLVRAY: How do you like it then?

CLARA: It's extraordinary.

GILLVRAY: It's an independent outfit, of course. Our job is to formulate policy ideas. And then sell them to the Party. We're independent. But we're terribly close.
(*He smiles and gestures* CLARA *towards some double doors which give on to the other half of the room, which is now revealed. Six desks in a circle with television monitors, VHS machines and computer terminals, all manned by girls taking notes. Piles of newspapers and magazines around them. The room is dark, artificially lit, like a fish tank.* GILLVRAY *points things out to* CLARA.)
This is something we've got pretty good at. It's our media watch. We're always on the look out for bias. They know we're watching. It means we have evidence when we want to prove preferential treatment.
(CLARA *smiles at a woman who is watching* Donald Duck.)
And we're always poised for a right of reply.
(*He touches the shoulder of one of the girls.* CLARA *notices.*)

INT. GILLVRAY'S OFFICE. EVENING
The office is almost bare but for an antique desk which contrasts with the other, modern furnishings. At the far end, there is an avant-garde sofa on which CLARA *is sitting, her legs stretched out in front of her.* GILLVRAY *is behind his desk.*
GILLVRAY: Does it interest you?
CLARA: What?
GILLVRAY: Work in communication.
CLARA: Oh, yes. Very much.
GILLVRAY: I'd love you to be my deputy here.
(CLARA *looks at him, not answering. He has a bowl of fruit in front of him, and now he picks up a peach, testing it for ripeness with his finger.*)
I have a series of theories about women.
CLARA: Oh, really?
GILLVRAY: It's my next book. I've done the family. Now I'm doing this. You know, nowadays people pretend we're all the same. But we're not. Are we?
(*He waits, but* CLARA *does not answer.*)
No, what's exciting is now different we are. (*He smiles.*)

66

Finally – women's behaviour – their attitudes, their gestures, their clothes – everything – express a fundamental need to submit.

CLARA: Submit?

GILLVRAY: Uh-huh.

(*His thumb goes through the skin of the peach.*)

CLARA: Well, what a theory.

GILLVRAY: Not fashionable.

CLARA: No. Is that what I'd do? If I worked here? Submit?

GILLVRAY: If that would please you.

CLARA: I see. Would I be paid as well?

(*He smiles at her joke.*)

GILLVRAY: Oh, very good. You're quick. I always knew we'd get on.

EXT. LONDON SQUARE. EVENING

The front door of the Georgian house. GILLVRAY *seen in the doorway saying goodbye to a couple of secretaries, then setting off cheerfully down the smart London street. Unobserved, on the other side of the square, among the trees,* CLARA *is watching and now starts to follow him.*

EXT. WHITEHALL. EVENING

GILLVRAY *making his way up Whitehall against the flow of late-evening commuters, all coming in the opposite direction. A self-absorbed and airy figure.* CLARA *following, unseen, twenty paces behind.*

EXT. LONDON CLUB. EVENING

The monumental doors of a large London club. Greek statues above the portico and top-hatted porters at the door, as GILLVRAY *bounds up the steps.*

EXT. LONDON STREET. EVENING

CLARA *heads for a red telephone box opposite the club and goes in. She riffles quickly through a telephone directory. Then she dials. We see her point of view. Across the road, through the window of the club, you can see a* PORTER *go across to* GILLVRAY, *who now comes towards the window to answer the*

telephone. *He has his back to us. As* CLARA *speaks he is
suddenly very still.*
CLARA: I know what you're doing.
　　(*There's a pause.*)
GILLVRAY: (*Voice over*) Hello. Who is this?
CLARA: I know who you are.
　　(*Another silence.*)
GILLVRAY: (*Voice over, hesitantly*) Who is this? Clara?
　　(*At once, her suspicions confirmed,* CLARA *throws down the
　　phone in a fury and opens the door, leaving the phone off the
　　hook. She runs fast across the road and up the steps of the
　　club.*)

INT. LONDON CLUB. EVENING
CLARA *coming through the high door of the club. At once the*
DOORMAN *attempts to stop her, with an 'Excuse me, please'.
She goes straight on into the hall. There is now panic, a couple of
porters running from other directions to intercept her, but she
heads on into the main clubroom. About thirty men are sitting
about in high-backed chairs, with drinks before dinner. There are
now five or six porters running towards her as she charges across
the room towards* GILLVRAY *who is still standing, holding the
dead phone.*

68

PORTER: Madam. No women are allowed in here.
(*In the clubroom now men are standing. At the sound of the*
PORTER'S *voice,* GILLVRAY *turns, his face red, sweating,*
horrified at the sight of CLARA *in front of him.*)
CLARA: I thought this was a gentleman's club. This isn't a
gentleman.
(*She stands, furious, triumphant, the whole room stilled. No*
one dares go near her. GILLVRAY *looks around, very quiet.*)
GILLVRAY: She has no sense of humour.
(*He puts his hand on her arm to try and get her from the*
room and she brushes him off violently. GILLVRAY *stands a*
moment, attempting schoolboy charm.)
I never see why women can't take a joke.

EXT. RIVER. DAY
At once Michael Swanton's corpse crashes over a small lock and
into the side of a boat where two men are fishing. The crash, as it
hits the side.

INT. FLAT. DAY
GERALD *in his pyjamas in the deserted flat reaches down for the*
morning paper. He opens it at the breakfast table. A small item:
ENGLISHMAN FOUND IN THE RIVER SEINE. *He looks up,*
thinking.

INT. ZINYAFSKIS' APARTMENT. DAY
WALLACE *at the kitchen table with a French newspaper. A big*
bowl of milky coffee in front of him. In the paper a tiny item,
bottom of the page. He has a pen. He circles the name 'Swanton'
in the story. Then taps his pen.

INT. BIRMINGHAM HALL. NIGHT
CLARA *is sitting in the darkness, a streak of light across her face.*
A man's hand on her shoulder.
ASSISTANT: It's this way.
(*She gets up and follows him. A man's hand lifts the curtain*
and we understand we are in the wings of a stage. He has a
brown suit and a Midlands accent. She is being led across
the stage towards the main curtain, and we begin to pick up
the sound of speech from in front of the curtain.)

SPEAKER: (*Voice over*) The newly chosen candidate in the forthcoming parliamentary election for Birmingham South West – where she was born . . . politician . . . mother . . . businesswoman and our future MP, ladies and gentlemen, Mrs Clara Paige.
(*Her face as she waits a moment, darkened, then the curtain is parted and she smiles.*)

INT. BIRMINGHAM HALL. NIGHT
We now see the scale of the meeting. Two hundred people on hard chairs, which have been set out in the grand rococo surroundings of Birmingham Town Hall. CLARA *is in mid-speech, high as a kite, to a rapt audience. A hot, smoky, high-rhetoric atmosphere.*
CLARA: I think everyone wonders, those of you who know me, who've been with me, you look at me and think, oh yes, there's Clara, always there, always confident, perhaps you think, no doubt she does a good job in Europe. But Europe's easy. How will she do at

Westminster? That's the big test. (*She smiles, low key, before the kill.*) Well, yes, it's different. Of course, it's harder. More intense, I'm ready for that. I'm looking forward to it. Because, you know, I think in a way, you have chosen me because we all share a feeling that we're sick up to here with guff and double-talk and compromise. People are crying out to be led. (*She pauses a second, a little overwhelmed.*) Oh yes, I'll always consult, I'll always want to know what you think, what you feel. But *once* I know, I think you deserve strong decisive leadership. And as your representative in Parliament, I think I can promise you that's what I'll provide.

(*At once the whole hall erupts. She sits down.*)

INT. BIRMINGHAM HALL. NIGHT
A lap of honour as CLARA *passes through the hall, acknowledging the warmth of everyone's greeting. She glad-hands her way through, flushed with her triumph, a glint of mad excitement in her eye.*

INT. BIRMINGHAM HALL: CORRIDOR. NIGHT
CLARA *walks down the corridor talking excitedly to the* CHAIRMAN, *in a group of six or seven people all talking about how well the occasion has gone. They pass the open door of a kitchen where tea and biscuits are being prepared. As they pass, a* WOMAN *behind the tea counter looks up. She catches* CLARA's *eye.*
WOMAN: Oh, Mrs Paige.
(CLARA *looks a moment, then smiles at her companions and says, 'Excuse me.' She goes into the kitchen. The* WOMAN *is in a Crimplene two-piece. She is in her late thirties, dowdy, lower-middle class. She is* JANET SWANTON.)
CLARA: Janet, well goodness.
JANET: How nice of you to remember me.
CLARA: Don't be ridiculous.
JANET: That was a really nice speech.
(CLARA *looks at her for a moment.*)
CLARA: I just heard about Michael, I'm sorry.

71

JANET: I just want things to go on as normal. That's why I
thought I'd come and help out today.
(*She stands a moment, tearful.* CLARA *waits.*)
Jenny said you were ever so kind to her. She wanted to
thank you but she couldn't find you.
CLARA: No. I had to go home.
(*The men are at the door waiting for this strange
conversation to be over. But* CLARA *stands, patiently.*)
JANET: You know, in funny way, I shouldn't say this, it's a
blessing. Jenny got a great job in Italy. Michael, you
know, he wasn't a happy man. Not for years. He'd been
in agony. The odd thing is . . . now they've found him
. . . we feel at peace.
(CLARA *is looking at her, still flushed, moved. She moves in
and kisses* JANET *on the cheek.*)
CLARA: I'm glad. I don't mean for Michael. But I'm glad for
everyone else.

INT. BIRMINGHAM HALL. NIGHT
CLARA *heads off with the committee away from the tea room
where she has just seen* JANET. *She has an air of deep inner
contentment. The committee are still chattering excitedly around
her.*
CHAIRMAN: That was fantastic. You must be very happy.
CLARA: I've never been happier.
CHAIRMAN: People like you up here. They like the way you
talk. They understand you.
CLARA: Good. I like them as well.
(*Round the marbled corner comes the* ASSISTANT *who
collected her for her speech.*)
ASSISTANT: Will you be driving back to London?
CLARA: I think I've earned a break.
(*The little circle of men smiles, as if this were
understatement.*)
I'm going to stay the night at my hotel.

INT. BIRMINGHAM HOTEL. NIGHT
*Seen from high above, the entrance to a large Victorian hotel, a
shaft of light falling on to the tarmac outside it.* CLARA's

*confident figure, seen from on top, as she walks through the light
and on into the doorway.*

INT. BIRMINGHAM HOTEL: CORRIDOR. NIGHT
CLARA *is walking alone down the darkened corridor of an
enormous Gothic provincial hotel. She is returning to her room. It
is very dark in the corridor, a bare light bulb throwing inadequate
light from the stairs at the end. As she comes to the door of her
room, she puts her hand on the handle and finds the door already
open. She stops, puzzled. She pushes the door open.*

INT. BIRMINGHAM HOTEL: BEDROOM. NIGHT
*She stands at the doorway. The bedroom is totally dark, but for a
ring of light around the bathroom door. She stands a moment,
terrified. She reaches for the light switch. It clicks, but no light
comes on. Realizing why not, she heads now for the bedside
control, but before she gets there, the bathroom door opens. Light
from the door. A man's shadow, quite still for a moment. Then*
WALLACE *steps into the light.*
WALLACE: I was in the audience. Loyal admirer.
CLARA: Wallace.
> (*She clicks on the bedside light. As she does,* WALLACE
> *throws an object in his hand down on the bed between them.
> It is her handbag.*)
WALLACE: There it is. Take it.
CLARA: I'd given it up. I bought another.
> (*Now she puts hers down on the bed, beside the one he has
> thrown down. They are absolutely identical, the original
> with all its contents intact. They sit there a moment, side by
> side.*)
> Have you come to see me? Why didn't you tell me you
> were coming?
> (*He just looks at her, not answering.*)
> I couldn't phone you. Because of Gerald. It's been
> torture. I've missed you.
WALLACE: Oh, really?
CLARA: It's wonderful to see you. How did you get in?
> (*They are standing on opposite sides of the bed, she flustered,*

improvising, trying to think what to say, he absolutely steady in his gaze.)

WALLACE: I read about your ex-partner.

CLARA: Oh God, yes, it was awful.

WALLACE: They fished him out of the Seine.

(CLARA *does not answer.*)

I see now why you were so hysterical that night.

CLARA: What do you mean?

(WALLACE *smiles.*)

WALLACE: Do you know where the police found the bag? On the Pont des Arts. It hadn't been stolen. It was handed in.

(*He looks at her. She doesn't react.*)

Go on, say.

CLARA: What?

WALLACE: Anything.

CLARA: Like what?

WALLACE: React. 'How extraordinary. I didn't go that way.'

CLARA: Well, I didn't.

WALLACE: Quick. Quicker, Clara. Think up a new lie. Improvise. You're meant to be smart.

(*She backs away a step, realizing he knows.*)

You've committed a crime. Insulting the intelligence. It

ought to carry ten years.

(*She looks at him a moment, making a decision, changing her tone.*)

CLARA: Look, all right, I'll tell you. How much do you know? I honestly believed Swanton was following me. He'd tried to blackmail me, or so I thought. Also, worse, there'd been some calls. (*She pauses a second.*) I tipped him over. It was an impulse. I so wanted to tell you before.

(WALLACE's *look does not waver.*)

Look, my darling, it was crazy. I admit it. You can't imagine what I've been through. I'm not a killer. I won't kill again. I made an honest mistake. For which I'm always going to suffer.

WALLACE: Inside?

CLARA: Yes. Isn't inside enough?

(WALLACE *smiles bitterly.*)

WALLACE: What you say about murder is what makes you so English. You told me once people should answer for their actions, whether they speak in a posh voice or not.

(CLARA *begins to panic slightly.*)

CLARA: What are you saying? You haven't been to the police?

(*He shakes his head.*)

Think about it. The whole thing is over. There were no witnesses. I have a son. Think what would happen to him if I went to prison. And Gerald. He's not a bad man. He just got in a mess, financially, and he chose a silly way out of it. These things happen, that's all. And you . . . why should *you* be justice? Why should it be you who weighs these things in the scales? It's not right. You'd always be sorry. Bury it. Honestly, you must.

(*She is pleading with him, but he does not move towards her.*)

WALLACE: You're corrupt. You have no character. That's your real curse. Words come out, but there's nothing in you.

CLARA: It's not true.

WALLACE: You're lost if there's no agenda. And there's no agenda tonight.

CLARA: That's not true. Why do you think I came to your flat? In the middle of the night, after I'd killed him? I came because I needed you. It was the most terrible risk. (*She pauses a moment.*) I came because I loved you.

WALLACE: Don't be ridiculous.

CLARA: Oh, I didn't know, not then . . .

WALLACE: You just needed company.

CLARA: Yes. At the start. I needed help. But later, no, it was real.

(*He moves round the bed, confident.*)

WALLACE: I came tonight because I wanted to be sure. I've been used.

CLARA: No.

WALLACE: You can't *use* people.

(*He suddenly has raised his voice at her, and now as he tries to leave, she flings herself against him, with violence. He drags her across the room. She wraps her arms round him and pleads with him.*)

CLARA: Wallace, please no, I need you, don't go. I'll care for you, I promise. There is a different side to me. That's what you once said. Don't you remember? A side of me that's decent. You said it. Remember?

(*She takes hold of him, trying to force him to look at her.*)

Please look at me, darling. Can't you see? Look into my eyes. Look at me. How can I be lying? That whole side of me's bound up in you.

(*He moves away, reluctant, confused.*)

You know there's some *good*. You know that there's good in me.

WALLACE: (*Very quietly*) I've been offered a job.

CLARA: Where?

WALLACE: In Burma. (*He smiles.*) They need my light fittings.

(*At once they both laugh at the ludicrousness of it all. The phone rings suddenly beside the bed, startlingly loud, cutting right through the room.* CLARA *looks at* WALLACE.)

CLARA: Answer it, please, I can't answer it.

(WALLACE *walks to the phone and lifts it up.*)

VOICE: Hello.

WALLACE: Yes. Who is it?
> (*There is silence at the other end.* WALLACE, *puzzled, holds the receiver away from his ear.*)
> (*To* CLARA) It's a man. (*Into phone*) Hello. Hello.
> (CLARA *watches a moment, then impulsively walks across the room and wrenches the receiver from* WALLACE *and shouts hysterically into the phone.*)

CLARA: Stop calling me. Will you ever stop calling me? I've told you stop calling me. Will you never leave me alone?

INT. FLAT: SITTING ROOM. NIGHT
GERALD is sitting alone on a darkened sofa in the sitting room. He puts the phone down just as CLARA *completes her sentence. He sits a moment in the chair, his face totally impassive.*

INT. BIRMINGHAM HOTEL: CORRIDOR. NIGHT
CLARA *and* WALLACE *coming together down the deserted Victorian corridor of the hotel.*

CLARA: Come on, let's get going.

WALLACE: Right now?

CLARA: Yes, of course. Let's do it. Come on, Wallace.
> (*He is hanging back.*)

WALLACE: Are you sure?
> (*He has stopped in the corridor. She goes back and takes his hand.*)

CLARA: Just come with me.
> (*They come round the next corner now, hand in hand, her leading.*)
> We'll drive together to London. When we get there, we'll tell Gerald everything.

WALLACE: Clara. You must tell him what you did.

CLARA: I will. And about us. He wants a divorce just as much as I do.
> (*She has turned the next corner. When* WALLACE *turns she has gone. He stands a moment. Then her voice.*)
> Wallace . . .
> (*He spins round. She is standing in the open doorway of a deserted ballroom. She puts her hand on his shirt, the palm*

77

*flat against him. She presses her body against his. They kiss.
The ballroom beyond.* WALLACE *looks into her eyes.*)

WALLACE: All right.

CLARA: It's time to be honest. If we're honest, we can make
a fresh start.

INT. FLAT. NIGHT

GERALD *gets up from the chair and goes from the room, without
turning the light on. He goes into the bedroom and reaches up to
the highest shelf for a cigar box in his wardrobe. He gets it down
and opens it. Inside, a revolver. He gets it out. He stands a
moment in the darkened bedroom. Then he moves into the corridor
and opens the door of Simon's room.* SIMON *in close-up asleep on
the pillow.* GERALD *moves across and lifts the boy up, wrapping
him in a blanket as he does.* SIMON *stirs.*

GERALD: It's all right.

    (GERALD *carries him in his arms away down the darkened
    corridor.*)

EXT. BIRMINGHAM HOTEL. NIGHT

*Clara's car parked in front of the hotel. Seen from an immense
height,* WALLACE *standing on one side as* CLARA *goes round the
back to put her luggage in the boot. She slams it closed, then
moves round to the open door and gets in.* WALLACE *is still
standing fifteen feet away by himself, the passenger's door also
open.*

EXT. PAULINE'S HOUSE. NIGHT

PAULINE *coming bewildered to the door in her dressing-gown.*
GERALD *standing outside with* SIMON *asleep in his arms.*

PAULINE: Gerald?

GERALD: Yes.

PAULINE: It's two thirty.

GERALD: I know. I'm sorry. Parliamentary business. I can't
tell you what. Do you think you could take care of the
boy?

PAULINE: When will you be back?

GERALD: Clara will be back in the morning.

    (SIMON *stirs and looks up.*)

SIMON: Daddy.
GERALD: It's fine.
(*He reaches down and kisses him.*)

INT. CLARA'S CAR. NIGHT
CLARA *on the motorway. She is driving at full speed, the
motorway signs flashing by, lights playing on her face.* WALLACE
*sitting impassive, silent beside her. She has pushed in a cassette.
The music is very loud.*

INT. FLAT. NIGHT
GERALD *comes back into the flat, stands a moment in the
corridor, motionless. He takes the gun from his pocket. Then
holding it in his hand he moves into the sitting room, and
positions a chair immediately behind the door. He sits down in the
dark.*

EXT. LONDON STREET. DAWN
The deserted street outside the mansion block. CLARA *draws the
car up outside.*

WALLACE: Do you want me with you?
CLARA: No. Just wait here.

INT. FLAT. DAWN
GERALD *sitting alone. The sound of the lift in the distance. He*
turns.

INT. LIFT. DAWN
CLARA *in the little Victorian cage as it slides up the middle of the*
building. She gets out, her shoes squeaking on the lino.

INT. FLAT. DAWN
GERALD *still sitting. The sound of the front door opening.* CLARA
comes into the sitting room. She puts her bag down. Then puts a
lamp on. She does not see him.
GERALD: You killed Swanton.
    (*She turns, startled.*)

81

CLARA: Gerald . . .

GERALD: You're having an affair.

(She looks confused, begins to move towards him.)

CLARA: Listen . . .

GERALD: You think you can get away with anything. No regard at all for anyone's feelings but your own. You're trash. You're just trash. You're human trash. And trash belongs in the dustbin.

(He has taken the gun from his pocket. It's there in his hand, pointing down. CLARA *panics.)*

CLARA: You stupid man, you pig-stupid man. Why did you write him a letter? Putting the figures down? How could you? How could you do anything so incredibly stupid?

GERALD: Because that's what I'm like. I'm weak. And don't think of the consequences.

(He lifts the gun, pointing it at his own head. But then he turns it towards her and fires. A tremendous blast, which hits her in the chest and throws her against the wall. He fires four more times at her. Blood and bones against the wall. She reels like a puppet with each shot.)

EXT. PAULINE'S HOUSE. DAY

SIMON, *asleep, stirs slightly.*

EXT. CLARA'S CAR. DAY
WALLACE *looks up, hearing the sound. He frowns, shrugging it off.*

INT. FLAT. DAY
CLARA *slumps to the ground, dead.*

EXT. CLARA'S CAR. DAY
On the seat beside WALLACE *is Clara's handbag, open where she has left it. Sticking out of the top is a napkin.* WALLACE *reaches down for it. There is his drawing of Clara's face. He opens the napkin. On the other side of it, she has drawn his, asleep in the bed in Paris. He looks up.*

INT. PAULINE'S HOUSE. DAY
SIMON *wakes up. Sits up. Listens.*